THE RIO SAN JUAN
Travels Along The Nicaragua Waterway

GILLIAN LYTHGOE
AND
JOE BROWN

Copyright © 2012 by Gillian Lythgoe and Joe Brown

All rights reserved. No part of this publication may be reproduced or transmitted in any form or by any means, electronic or mechanical, including photocopy, recording, or any information storage and retrieval system, without permission in writing from the copyright owner.

ISBN 978-1478335801

Printed in the United States of America

For

Joe Brown

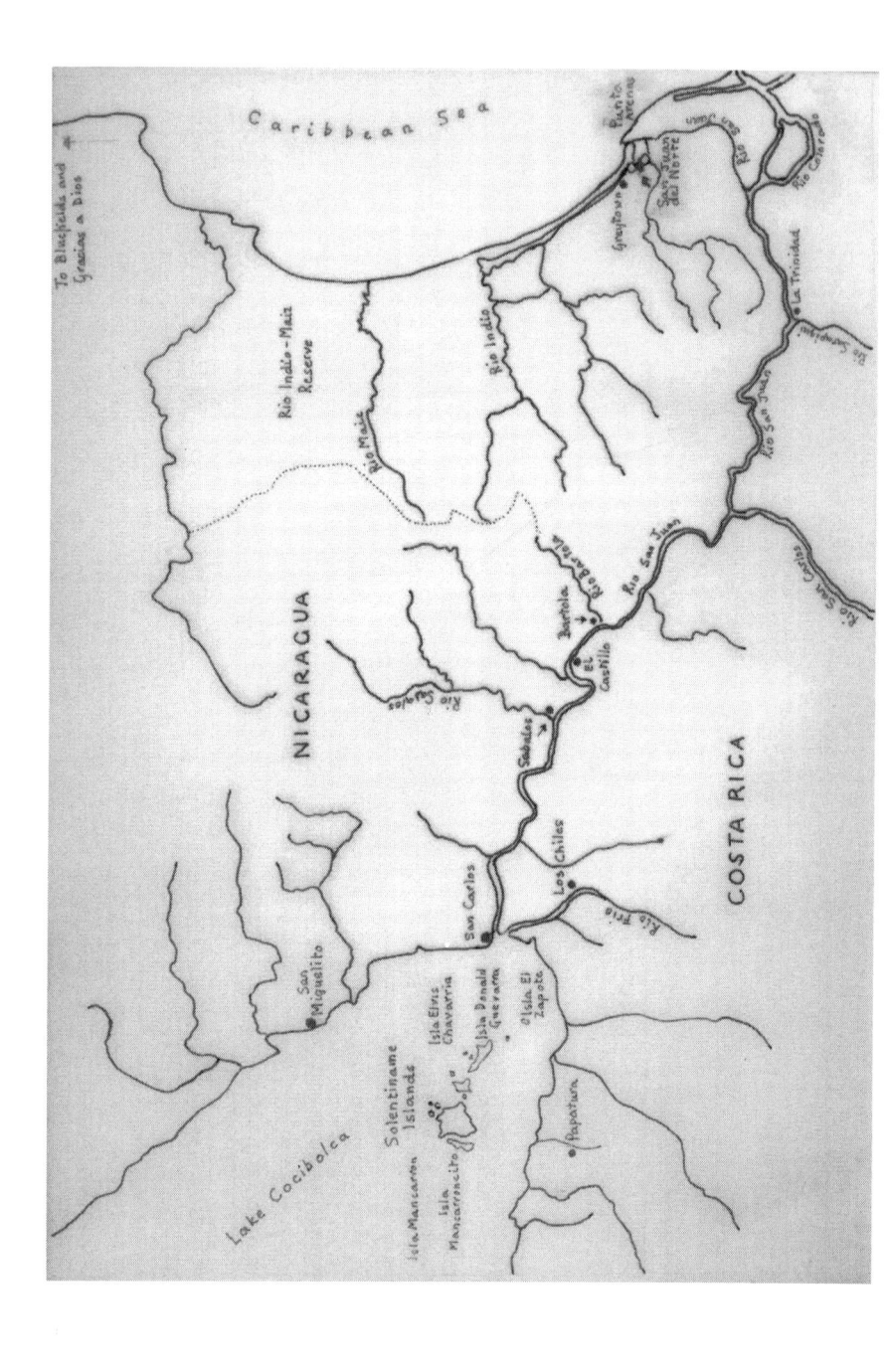

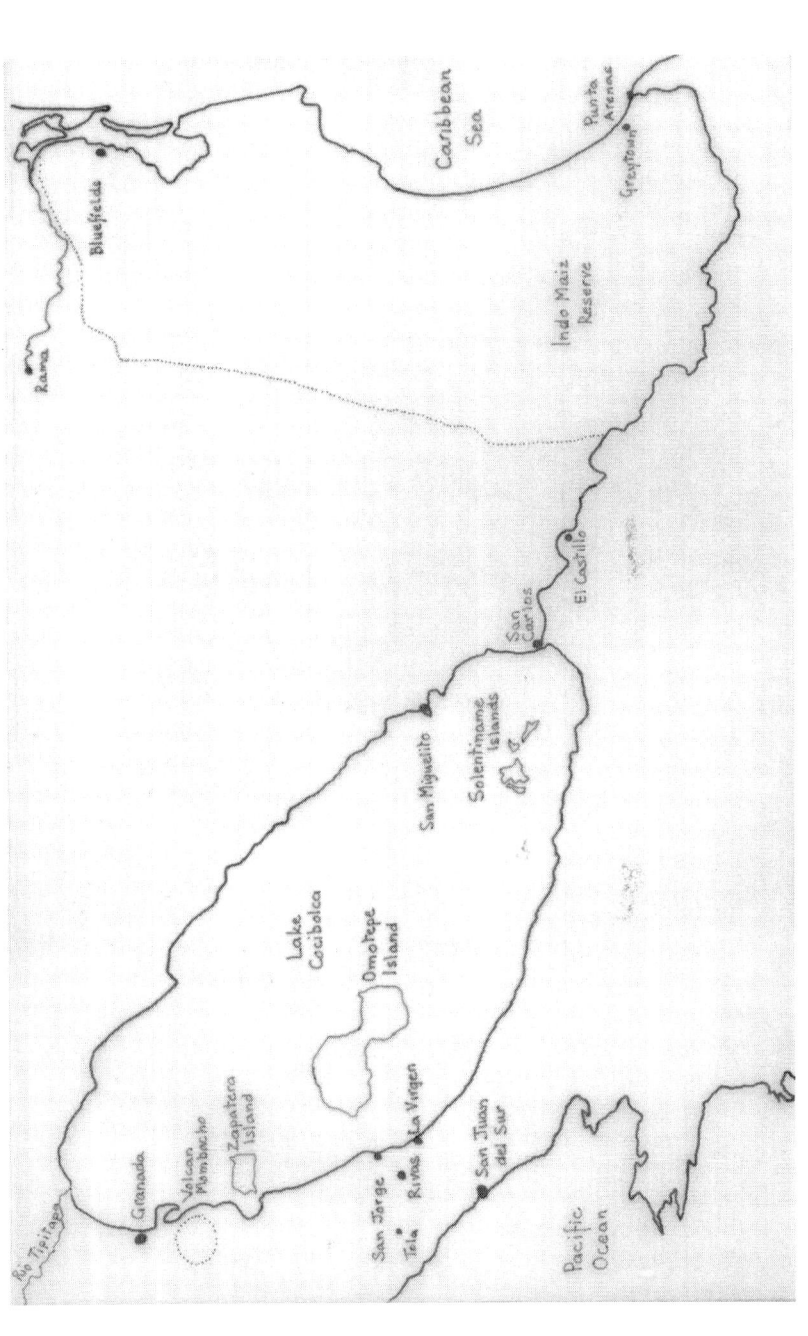

CONTENTS

Acknowledgements
Introduction
Confusing Names
Measurements
Dates
Chapter 1 Dreams of a River
Chapter 2 Granada
Chapter 3 Volcanoes, Discovery and Conquistadores
Chapter 4 Lake Cocibolca
Chapter 5 Granada to San Carlos
Chapter 6 Early Explorers
Chapter 7 San Carlos to Sábalos
Chapter 8 Reaching the Atlantic
Chapter 9 Sábalos to El Castillo
Chapter 10 The Spanish, Pirates and the British on the River
Chapter 11 El Castillo and El Diablo
Chapter 12 Bartola to Trinidad
Chapter 13 The Lower Rio San Juan
Chapter 14 River Squabbles
Chapter 15 The Gold Rush and William Walker
Chapter 16 Omotepe
Chapter 17 River Battles
Chapter 18 Greytown and The Bar
Chapter 19 New Greytown
Chapter 20 Early River Travellers
Chapter 21 Vanderbilt and Isthmus Traffic
Chapter 22 The Decline of the River
Chapter 23 Canals
Chapter 24 Up the River and Solentiname
Chapter 25 Papatura
Addendum
Appendices
Bibliography

ACKNOWLEDGEMENTS

I am not sure that I would have finished the manuscript of this book without the encouragement of my daughters, Charlotte & Katrina, Bill and Penny Ashman in Granada who are going to end up with copies of the book cluttering their beautiful house. Thanks must go to Jean Hartley, Doug and Beverly Tyler and Jenny George who all read the manuscript and gave many helpful suggestions. I must also thank Roberto for his tremendous hospitality in Solentiname and some memorable evenings. Last, the amazing British Library in London where Joe and I both spent time pouring over wonderful old books from where we were able to glean some of our information.

Gillian Lythgoe

Hernán Cortéz   In a letter to King Carlos I of Spain:

"He who possesses the Rio San Juan could be considered the owner of the world."

Rio San Juan

INTRODUCTION

In 2005, Joe Brown a 71year old Texan farmer, rancher and balloon pilot and Gillian Lythgoe a retired 63 year old from London, England, took a trip in Joe's classic 1979 double-ended 17 foot aluminium Grumman canoe with a 2½hp motor down the San Juan river in Nicaragua from San Carlos on lake Cocibolca to New Greytown near the Atlantic Ocean. Joe had used the canoe only once before, in Idaho in 1978, and his second time was our experiment with it on a lake on Joe's ranch in Texas; my very first canoe experience.

We took the canoe down the Rio San Juan and when we returned from the trip we started to tell friends about our experience and after we had repeated the stories a dozen times, we decided that the best thing would be to try to write it all down.

Writing about the trip and learning about the river became almost an obsession so, intertwined with our canoe trip, are tales of other peoples who had travelled the river; ancient people, early Europeans, pirates and filibusters; and tales of the trees and animals.

Prior to our trip down the San Juan, Joe had travelled the river on his own and later we both explored the Solentiname Islands and Papatura. Joe made further trips to these islands, San Carlos and Sábalos as well as the islands of Omotepe and Zapatera and information gleaned on these trips has also been included.

This is our tale of
the River San Juan
and the Nicaraguan waterway.

CONFUSING NAMES

Some of the nomenclature used in this book may be confusing. We hope that the following will help.

Lake Cocibolca

In 1521 when Gil Gonzáles Dávila saw the great lake, he called it the Mar Dulce. But the lake already had a name, Cocibolca and it was this name that was in common use. Today, the lake is often called Lake Nicaragua and this is the name found on most maps but, as the people who live around the lake today still call it Lake Cocibolca, we chose to use this name for the lake.

Greytown

The first settlement in the lagoon at the mouth of the Rio San Juan near the Atlantic Ocean was called San Juan del Norte or San Juan de Nicaragua. In 1848 the name was changed to Greytown. The town that now exists, on a different site but near the original town is, again, called San Juan del Norte. However, there is a movement in the town to get the name changed to New Greytown and, as this is the name that the local population want for their town, it is the name that we have used.

Steamships

There is plenty of scope for confusion around the names of the steamships as many of them were named after settlements along the San Juan and around the lake. The context should make it obvious whether the name refers to a ship or a place.

Political Parties

The two rival political parties in Nicaragua, for much of the time that we talk about were the democrats or liberals based in Leon and the conservatives or legitimists based in Granada. We have used the terms democrat and conservative to identify these two parties but these titles bear only some resemblance to our understanding of the terms today.

Misquito Indians

Living along the Atlantic Coast of Central America including Nicaragua and the Mosquito Coast are Indians, often referred to as Mosquito Indians. Misquito is probably a more accurate name but both will be used in the book.

Literature

Our information was sourced from many publications and sometimes the facts were quite contradictory. We did not attempt to unravel the threads within the literature, we have left that to the academics. We have tried to keep to the majority view but have sometimes included alternative versions.

MEASUREMENTS

1 metre	= 3.28 feet
1 foot	= 0.304 metres
1 vara square	= 0.70 metres square
1 acre	= 0.405 hectares
1 hectare	= 2.47 acres
1 manzana	= 1.73 acres
1 manzana	= 10,000 varas square
1 hectare	= 10,000 metres square
1 flete of cane	= 42 rolls of cane (though this can be variable) each containing 25 pieces of cane 2 1/2 to 3 metres in length

Rio San Juan

DATES

There are a lot of dates in the book and following is brief chronological list of some of the events that occurred in and which I hope may prove useful, particularly during the periods when a lot of different things were going on at the same time, for example during the Vanderbilt/ Walker/ canal period.

60 million years ago	Nicaragua emerged
20,000.00 BC	Mombacho exploded
8,000.00 BC	A coastal community on the Atlantic
6,000.00 BC	Human footprints
2,000.00 BC	Early human artifacts
1,200.00 AD	Chorotega and Nicarao tribes arrived
1492 October 12th	Colombus landed on the Bahamas
1502 September 12th	Colombus landed on Nicaragua
1513	Pedrarias D'Avila sent by Spain to the Americas
1513 September 25th	Vasco Nuñez de Bálboa sees the Pacific
1519	Hernán Cortéz landed in Mexico
1521	Gil Gonzáles Dávila sees the lake and names it Mar Dulce
1522	Francisco Hernández de Córdoba sent to Nicaragua and founded Granada
1522	Gil Gonzáles Dávila found the outlet from the lake of the river
1525	Díaz first foreigner to travel along part of the river

1529	Martín Estete gave the river the name San Juan
1539 July 24th	Alonso Calero navigates the river
1551	Probably the first canal proposal
1571	Francis Drake in Panama
1602	Fort Santa Cruz at El Castillo
1660's	500 buccaneers living near the mouth of the San Juan and pirates controlling the mouth.
1663	Earthquake stopped navigation by the big ships
1665	Fort built at San Carlos
1665 June 29th	John Davis and Henry Morgan sack Granada
1675	Fort El Castillo de la Inmaculada Concepción completed
1727	12 garrisons along the San Juan
1745	El Castillo the only San Juan garrison
1762	Rafaela Herrara saves El Castillo
1780	Nelson on the San Juan
1781	First serious canal proposal
1821 October 3rd	Nicaragua independence
1823	Monroe Doctrine drafted
1825	Central American Federation formed
1838	CAF collapses
1841	British Marines take San Juan del Norte
1848	San Juan del Norte changed to Greytown
1848	Gold discovered in California
1849	First organised San Juan voyage
1849	Vanderbilt gets a charter for the Pacific Ship Canal Co.
1850	The first steamship to navigate the waterway
1850	Clayton-Bulwer Treaty

1851 First regular passenger service
1852 Vanderbilt survey for a canal
1855 June William Walker arrives in Nicaragua
1856 Costa Rica at war with Nicaragua
1856 July 12th Walker becomes President
1857 San Juan in Costa Rican hands
1857 December 15th Walker leaves Nicaragua
1868 Thomas Belt in Nicaragua
1878 DeLessups starts building Panama Canal
1889 Construction starts on Nicaraguan Canal
1901 Panama gets canal decision
1990 New Greytown built

Chapter 1. Dreams of a River

Rain falls in the forested highlands of Nicaragua and the merging waters stream down to the mighty Lake Cocibolca and stroll the 160 kilometres of its length until they tumble into the Rio San Juan, a route of beauty, bloodshed and political machinations that leads to the Atlantic Ocean.

Joe and I sat on traditional carved rocking chairs on the top terrace of our house in Granada, Nicaragua as we looked across the red tiled rooftops, mango trees and coconut palms towards Mombacho volcano. The temperature was 30 degrees centigrade with humidity to match. Ice cubes chunked in frosted glasses of Flor de Caña rum as we gazed at the evening clouds as they materialised above the humid rainforest. White and grey tinged with gold, pink and purple from the setting sun they swelled and climbed. Pushed by the evening winds away from the great lake they rolled along the ridge of Mombacho volcano.

Joe leant back, stretched his legs and in his Texas drawl said:
"Y'know that canoe we carried all the darned way here from Texas on top of the pick-up truck"?
"I should remember, I drove the truck." I replied.
"Well I think that this is the time for the Rio San Juan trip."
"Couldn't we wait until the end of the rainy season when it might not be quite so wet?" I remarked.
"No, I sure need a break from house building and now is as good a time as any."

Rio San Juan

In 1965 Joe, then aged 32, had worked on a farm in Nicaragua and during many evening conversations had heard about the San Juan, its forests and wildlife and the large number of jaguars. He had longed to travel the river and see it for himself and now he could realise his dream.

Some months earlier we had been in Texas packing things into two vehicles to take down to our newly bought house in Granada when, as we were deciding what we should or should not take, Joe looked at the Grumman canoe and said:

"I've had that canoe for twenty years and hardly used it. I want to do something special with it and I think that we ought to take it down the Rio San Juan. It has been sitting in this barn for all those years and we are now living on one of the greatest lakes in the world and ever since I first went to Nicaragua I have wanted to go down the Rio San Juan. The history of the river is exciting and it would be an adventure."

So the decision was made to take the canoe with us.

Joe decided that it was impracticable for us to paddle the canoe the whole way and that we ought to get a small 2½hp engine for the canoe, even though we were unsure whether the canoe would cope, get the canoe down from the barn roof and try it out.

We went shopping, found an engine and as the shop had a promotional sale of boat engines, and as Joe could never resist a bargain, a 6hp engine was purchased as well.

"Why do we need that?" I asked.

"Well, as we live on one of the largest areas of freshwater in the world, a bigger engine may just be useful.

We will also need to buy a spare propeller and shear pins in case we break them in the rapids."

"Rapids!" I almost shouted. "You didn't say anything about rapids, it is meant to be a big wide river with trees and birds and butterflies, not rapids." Suddenly, my view of the whole project had changed.

"Stop making a fuss, the rapids are nothing, just a short section and we can carry everything around them if necessary." Joe complacently replied.

"Then why do we need the spares?" I asked.

"Insurance." Was the short reply.

We left the shop with our new purchases, and as Joe had succumbed to stories of fish, he had also bought three new rods, plus reels, and lines, and lures. We gently cossetted the engine and rods in an old quilt in the back of the pick-up and headed back to the ranch.

Next day we unwrapped our purchases and Joe admired his new engine. I was trying to find a bracket that would fit the canoe and onto which we could attach the engine, but the information I was getting was very conflicting, one company said it was just not possible, it was a canoe and meant to be paddled not driven. At last, one company said, "yes you can attach an engine to the canoe, no problem, and we will sell you the bracket"! The bracket duly arrived and looked like something that Joe could have knocked up in half an hour with some of the spare bits out of the barn.

The barn was used for storing all that precious stuff that you don't have an immediate use for but it was also notorious as, some months earlier when some old bales of hay were being removed, over one hundred rattlesnakes and copperheads were caught! The canoe was suspended from the ceiling and we carefully lowered it down on its ropes, which turned out to be surprisingly easy as the canoe was light and manageable and, no signs of snakes.

We manhandled it onto the pick-up and drove down to the big tank. To any non-American and even to some of those, a tank is an artificial lake primarily used to water cattle, but pretty good for fishing. Early evening, the water had barely a ruffle and was so clear that you could see the weeds and fish from the surface. The cattle on the far side casually chewed and watched as the canoe, with its engine, slid into the water and even after 20 years it did not have a single leak.

Joe filled the tiny, 1 litre fuel tank, started the engine and was off for a few laps. Everything looked good, the silver boat gleamed in the evening light leaving barely a ripple behind. Back at the bank, Joe said:

"Get in, at the front, I need some ballast".

Funny how often I am used for ballast, particularly when we were ballooning. I cautiously got in, settled myself on a seriously uncomfortable seat and as the canoe was really, really unstable any little movement made it wobble. I consoled myself with the thought that I could always get out and swim but once the engine got going, it was better.

After some complicated laps and turns to see how fast it would go and how easily it would turn, the inevitable happened. I leant over too far, fell overboard and upturned the whole ensemble, canoe, engine and Joe. I surfaced to be greeted by a wet, thoroughly reproachful, Joe. Getting the canoe and engine upright was easy and we retrieved the paddles and made our way back to shore. In the final analysis, Joe declared the first voyage a success, particularly as the engine started like a 'bull out of a chute' first time after its dip. Joe now had visions of the Rio San Juan.

"OK let's go."

We had come to a pause in house restoration and could easily take off for two or three weeks to see more of the country and it was as good a time as any for the trip down the Rio San Juan.

The San Juan river is big, the second longest in Central America, 190 kilometres from Lake Cocibolca to the Atlantic. Three major rivers and 17 tributaries feed it and at some times of the year it can be 350metres wide. And we were going in our little canoe with its 2½ hp engine and some very uncomfortable aluminium seats.

"Is there any way we can make the seats a more comfortable?" I asked.

I had visions of us irritable, fidgety and sore after five hours sitting in a cramped space and it seemed like a recipe for an over-turned canoe.

Next day I found Joe with two plastic chairs of the type that can be hired by the hundreds here for weddings, funerals, preachers and parties, all delivered piled high in the back of a pick-up truck. Joe had cut the legs down so that they would fit over the existing seats and they were ideal. They worked perfectly in the boat, worth every second of the time and effort spent in adapting them.

Chapter 2.   Granada

Granada is inseparable from the story of the Rio San Juan. It sits 60 metres above sea level, one kilometre inland from the northwest corner of Lake Cocibolca and 157 kilometres from San Carlos at the other end of the lake where the Rio San Juan starts its journey.   Founded by Captain Francisco Hernándes de Córdoba on the 21st April 1524, it is the oldest, continuously inhabited, colonial town in the Americas.   Since then it has seen riches and revolution, pirates and pillage, buccaneers and filibusters.   In 1583 a religious procession in Granada was described as:

'…rich in gold, and emeralds with Indian dances that lasted without rest for the duration of the procession and a line of very well dressed Spaniards'.

This when the total Spanish population was around 200.   By 1633, when the gold miner and naturalist Thomas Gage visited he marvelled at its wealth, most of which had come through trade with Peru, Guatemala and Colombia.

Granada is dominated by Mombacho volcano, which with its jagged crown, keeps watch over the town. Its lower slopes are carpeted with coffee farms and at the top is a verdant, pristine, cloud and elfin forest that covers five craters with an extravaganza of life unique to the volcano. At last count it had reached 752 species of plants, including hundreds of orchids and bromeliads; 168 different birds, which include some parrots, flocks of which would fly chattering over our house each morning and evening on their daily trips. The 60 mammal species include at least one big cat, and three monkeys; spiders, white-faced and howlers of which over 100 troops roam the ranches and coffee plantations as well as the forest. There are 28 species of reptiles and 10 amphibians, including the endemic Mombacho salamander, and some 30,000 insects.

Mombacho must have been magnificent in its heyday, a perfect cone, similar to those of the beautiful Concepcion volcano on Omotepe island and Momotombo which dominates the scene as you approach Managua from Granada and called that:

'bald and nude colossus' by Victor Hugo and:

'the father of fire and stone' by Ruben Dario, the beloved poet of Nicaragua.

Mombacho stands 1345 metres high after erupting one tumultuous day some 20,000 years ago when the top third of the volcano exploded, hurling rocks and stones into the air, many of them landing in the lake to form Las Isletas, 354 small islands just south of Granada, whilst lava flowed from the crater to push into the lake and form a small promontory. Today, Mombacho is dormant, or rather, sleeping, as the guides at the reserve prefer.

Granada is a low-rise town of adobe houses with huge wooden doors and thick walls that conceal courtyards, gardens, fountains and pools. The exteriors are vibrantly painted in brilliant, cheerful colours, ours was yellow and pink whilst another was a two-tone purple and red.

The main square is surrounded by double-storey Colonial houses and hotels with pillared verandas and overlooked by the cheerful and welcoming golden yellow cathedral. The square is shady, the trees often noisy with garish parrots and the many benches occupied by old men talking and tourists deep into guidebooks whilst snacking on the fried pork-skins sold from kiosks. Children were selling cashew nuts or playing around the fountain of naked cherubs. One, Pablo, who when I asked him why he was not in school, assured me that he was going to school and that this was just, another, holiday but bounced off when he saw a potential tourist victim. Shoes were cleaned, chickens and platanos cooked and served on banana leaf plates. Pots and plates, beautifully decorated with animal and pre-Columbian designs, were laid out for sale by the potters from a nearby town. A huge Nicaraguan flag flew from the new flagpole and as everything has to be built with earthquakes in mind, the foundations of this pole go down some 10 feet and the flag is clearly expected to survive any catastrophe.

The streets of Granada are dominated by views of churches. Rather than restore everything, some of the blackened burnt facades, from the burning of Granada in 1856, have been retained and the frequent processions with statues, bands, dancing and extremely loud fireworks are part of everyday life and would be part of the entertainment for the following week's International Poetry Festival, where it is not uncommon to have some 500 people listening to poetry at 10 o'clock at night. The spirit of Ruben Dario lives on.

Horse drawn carriages stand outside the hotels for tourists to ride down the wide avenue to the lake, but they may also be found outside the market taking Granadanians home with their shopping. Building supplies currently delivered by horse and cart are gradually being replaced by trucks and will soon be part of history, which will be a big relief for the horses and not many people will miss the aroma of horse manure.

In the warm evenings there is a tradition for the doors of the houses to be open and chairs taken out onto the pavement where people talk and rock (every chair in Nicaragua is a rocking chair) and greet friends passing by. Walking down the street can be slow progress as it is expected that you stop and chat with everyone you know and some you don't, though an 'adios', a particularly engaging Spanish greeting given when someone is just passing by, will do. In the centre of the town it is almost mandatory that your wooden doors be open during the day so that tourists, in particular, can peep in and see the colonial style rooms with their high ceilings, tiled patterned floors, wicker and wooden furniture and glimpse the courtyard behind. The Granadanians are proud of their town and welcome the inquisitive glances, but the outer wrought iron doors remain firmly closed.

Granada's situation, founded on the bank of lake Cocibolca, was of such strategic, political and economic importance that it became the focus of many of the events that occurred in the country and around the lake and the Rio San Juan. One of the people who was drawn into the politics of the country was William Walker (about whom there will be much more later) and he immediately recognised the central importance of the town in maintaining a water route across Nicaragua, particularly as he believed that control of the lake was more important than control of the river and Granada was the key.

Chapter 3 Volcanoes, Discovery and Conquistadors

Nicaragua is in the centre of the Americas, it lies between 11 and 15 degrees north of the equator, and covers 127,849 sq. kilometres of land. It used to be more, but during its, often violent, relationships with its neighbours, lost 50,000 sq. kilometres, the Guanacaste and Nicoya peninsula to Costa Rica, about which things are still testy, and more land to Honduras.

It was the last piece of the central American landmass to slot into place some 60 million years ago when the land emerged from an energetic system of moving plates and powerful volcanoes that brought rocks, some over 200 million years old to the surface, to complete the land bridge between the north and south American continents and separate the Atlantic Ocean from the Pacific. The east emerged first and this land gradually eroded to form the low-lying Caribbean areas of today. Then, suddenly, a line of volcanoes appeared along the Pacific edge of Central America to form a second narrow landmass that left the Nicaraguan basin in between. This depression gradually filled with water until it eventually overflowed at a point somewhere near to where El Castillo is situated today. The course of the Rio San Juan gradually formed and the water escaped into the Caribbean. Today the outlet from the lake is several miles northwest of the original exit and fifty feet lower. This gradual lowering of water level led to the huge central lake partially draining and dividing to form the lakes Managua and Nicaragua. The total length of the rivers and their tributaries in Nicaragua is enormous, the Rio Coco in the north is the longest river in Central America whilst the Rio San Juan is the second longest. There are 15 crater lakes that include the two largest lakes in Central America,

Cocibolca and Managua. It was over these lakes and rivers that much blood would be spilt.

Nicaragua is traditionally known as 'the land of lakes and volcanoes' and sits on top of one of the most active plate systems in the world, 300 low level tremors a day have been recorded. A chain of forty impressive volcanoes have thrust into the sky, the youngest of which, Cerro Negro, emerged, to much amazement, in the middle of a field in the 1800s. Still growing, it is now 400 metres high and still erupting, smothering Leon in 15 centimetres of ash and dust in 1992. The land still shudders and shakes; volcanoes steam and spit, mud bubbles and occasionally, lava flows. Six volcanoes have been active in the last 100 years, the rest, sleeping.

One result of all this natural activity was ash and, together with other volcanic sediments, created an environment that was exceptionally fertile. The Spanish conquistadors reported

> '...that the Nicaraguan plains are some of the most beautiful and pleasant lands that can be found in the Indies because they are very fertile with ....fruits of many kinds and much cacao'.

This rich soil has also bestowed Nicaragua with some of the largest tracts of unspoilt land, some 5.5 million hectares, of broadleaf forest with an impressive diversity of life. 15-17,000 flowering plants and 9,000 vascular plants, many of which have medicinal uses. 1,804 vertebrates have been recorded, 21 of which are endemic, and the 176 mammals include six cats and three monkeys. There are 676 birds the spectacular blue-crowned mot-mot being adopted as the national bird, and 172 reptiles and 64

Rio San Juan

amphibians. So little work has been done on the insects that it is thought that only 1% of an estimated 250,000 species have been identified. Spend a couple of days looking and you will probably find a new one or two! The bad news is that although much of these areas are protected it is disappearing at a rate of 15,000 hectares each year. Many of the indigenous Indians living in these areas exist in abject poverty and rely on the forest for their sustenance and survival; it will only be by tackling their needs that the forest and its creatures will be more secure.

Once the new landmass joining the north and south was complete it allowed animals to move from north to south, and south to north, and develop into the eco-systems that exist today and, man moved too.

The geography and the huge natural resources of fresh water, fertile soil and two coastal regions are obvious reasons for the human occupation of Nicaragua. The earliest remains are from 8,000BC, from a shellfish eating community on the Atlantic Ocean. They are a mysterious people as all we know about them is that they did exist, where they lived, and what they ate. Human footprints from 2,000 years later have been found in Managua but with no artefacts, we may never learn more about these early people.

Around 1200AD the Chorotega and Nicarao tribes in Mexico moved south. fleeing the bloodthirsty Aztecs, and eventually came to Nicaragua where they remained. Three hundred years later when foreign powers were thirsting for the wealth of the Americas they were still there and fought for their lands against these foreign invaders.

It is not really known when the Americas were found but the word 'America' or something similar, was already in common usage by European sailors years before Columbus sailed into the Caribbean on October 12th 1492 and stepped ashore on the Bahamas. Cabot in the Matthew certainly reached somewhere around Newfoundland on 24th June 1497 when Columbus was still in the Caribbean but as he never returned from his last voyage his exploits are barely known and have been largely forgotten. The reality is that people had probably reached the Americas some time much earlier.

Columbus was born into a family of woollen weavers in Genoa in 1451. He grew to be tall, well-built, with a long face, alert blue eyes and an aquiline nose; his hair was red but by the time he had reached his 30th birthday it had turned grey. He was creative, a moderate drinker, a devoted Catholic and sponsored by Spain. Sailing west, his dream was to find a new route to the Orient. That was impossible but what he did find were the Caribbean Islands, including Jamaica and Hispaniola that later on were to become pirate centres and from where havoc was made on the Rio San Juan, and he found America, a continent totally new to the Spanish Crown.

Knowledge of the Americas had wetted appetites in Europe for exploration and, in 1502 on his fourth and last voyage, Christopher Columbus was charged to discover:

'in the Indies in the part that belongs to us',

islands and continents and to find products of gold, silver, pearls, precious stones and spices. Although he is commonly reported as being charged to find a navigable passage through the landmass, this was not the main reason of his voyage but, in a letter sent to Vasco de Gama, who was on his way to India by sailing east, was an oblique comment that:

'Don Cristóbal Cólon is sailing thither westward …and it may be that you will meet on your course.'

The sovereign was clearly hoping that a strait would be found across the Americas and that Columbus would have sailed around the world.

Columbus was 51 years old and suffering from arthritis when on the night of May 25th 1502 he set sail from the Canary Islands 'west and by south' in his ship known as La Capitana, captained by his loyal shipmate Diego Tristan, and three other caravels. The total crew of all four ships was 140 men, one quarter of whom did not see Spain again; they deserted, drowned, died of disease or were killed.

Twenty-one days after sailing they landed on Martinique where the crews recouped after the crossing, washed clothes, and themselves, and then continued on past Dominica, the Leeward Islands and Puerto Rico to Hispaniola where Columbus wanted to ride out an approaching hurricane. He had already experienced hurricanes and recognised the warning signs so, when he saw an armada of 30 sail about to leave the harbour for Spain, he sent the Governor a message suggesting that they wait, and also requested permission for his own ships to enter and anchor to ride out the storm. There was a long-standing disagreement between Columbus and Hispaniola and the governor ridiculed Columbus's message declaring that he was now 'a prophet and soothsayer'. The ships sailed and Columbus was refused permission to enter the harbour. Twenty of the armada ships were completely lost together with 500 men and one of the richest cargoes of gold was sent to the depths of the ocean. Only one ship made it back to Spain.

Columbus found a shelter and the four caravels anchored. All was well until the night when three of them were blown out into the raging storm with its foaming waves and screaming wind. La Capitana's anchor held, but only by strapping all available pieces of ironmongery on to the chain. The other caravels fought the storm and by amazing seamanship they all survived and made their way to a previously agreed rendezvous.

On they sailed past Jamaica, where Columbus had already missed Kingston harbour; past the Caymans and Cuba where there too he overlooked the two best anchorages. The weather was good and in three days they covered 360 miles to sight the island of Banacca off Honduras.

There he found a large dugout with 25 men, women and children, far more sophisticated than the naked Indians of the Caribbean islands. They had cotton clothes, shawls, wooden swords set with flints that cut like steel, copper utensils, grains, beer and chocolate beans. A short sail across to the mainland to where is now Trujillo, and Columbus took possession of the land for his sovereign and Spain whilst hundreds of Indians watched the ceremony and traded goods 'in a festive atmosphere'. People from many tribes were present at the ceremony and they made an impression with their designs of lions, deer and castles painted on their naked skin and large holes in their ear lobes 'large enough to insert a hen's egg' and 'faces painted red and black to appear beautiful, but really they look like devil's'. These Indians are now thought to be emigrants from a forest of South America.

The fleet now turned south along the coast in atrocious weather. Columbus recounts:

> 'It was one continual rain, thunder and lightning. The ships lay exposed to the weather, with sails torn, and anchors, rigging, cables, boats and many stores lost; the people exhausted. Other tempests I have seen but none that lasted so long or so grim as this.'

They were following the coast, tacking in extreme conditions, everybody working to the limit, soaking wet and

Rio San Juan

eating whatever food they could find, cooking was completely out of the question. Always watching for shoals, reefs and rocks they searched for river outlets and harbours that could be an entrance to a strait across the continent that would bring them fame and glory. During the 28 days of the storm, they sailed only 165-170 miles. His ships were in very real danger but on September 12th 1502 Columbus reached a headland, the weather improved and he named it Gracias de Dios. He had found Nicaragua.

On south they sailed, past Pearl Lagoon and Bluefields and on to Costa Rica, completely missing the mouth of the Rio San Juan. One writer suggests that Columbus did make landfall at the river mouth for water and supplies and to give the crew a rest. However, it seems very unlikely that if he had got into the estuary, that he did not explore and discover the river as this was, after all, one of the things that he was meant to be doing. The truth may simply be that as the sand bars across the harbour were constantly changing, he was fooled and simply missed the river mouth completely or, perhaps, he landed elsewhere.

The remainder of this fourth voyage was dramatic, it continued to be beset by the most terrible storms and one that lasted over a month off what is now Panama, included a waterspout.

'The tempest arose and wearied me...; my old wound opened up, and for nine days I was as lost without hope of life; eyes never beheld the sea so high, angry and covered with foam. Never did the sky look more terrible; for one whole day and night it blazed like a furnace, and the lightning broke forth with such violence that each time I wondered if it had carried off my spars and sails...All this time the water never ceased to fall from the sky; I don't say rained, because it was like a deluge. The people were so worn out that they longed for death to end their dreadful sufferings.'

The sailing had been so difficult and tortuous in the appalling conditions that when they were able to anchor, the exhausted men wanted and needed only rest, recuperation, and food to recover strength before tackling the repairs to the battered ships. It is understandable that they were not too interested in exploring the rivers, which was rather sad as, where they were anchored, was to become the entrance to the Panama Canal. But gold had been found and Columbus now concentrated on his main mission, to find wealth.

Columbus made it back to Spain but not before all his ships had to be abandoned as they were eaten up by teredo worms and he and his crews were marooned on Jamaica for over a year. He died in Spain on May 20th 1506.

Spain was still seeking riches and had sent others west to explore. Rodrigo de Bastidas landed in 1501 but while he found neither fame nor fortune, a member of his crew, Vasco Nuñez de Bálboa, did rather better. He was living in Santo Domingo, Hispaniola when he had to make a quick getaway to avoid debts so stowed away on a ship to Panama where he became part of a community of 800 compatriots. They soon dwindled to 60, and though terrified of the jungle animals, the snakes, cats and crocodiles they were unaware of the danger of mosquitoes. The very real killers were malaria and yellow fever. Bálboa took control of the despondent group. He befriended and traded with the Indians instead of slaughtering them. He gained their trust and ended up with a beautiful Indian chief's daughter as his mistress. On September 25th 1513, whilst searching for gold with his Indian friends, Bálboa became the first European to see the Pacific. The land bridge between the Atlantic and Pacific Oceans had been discovered.

Rio San Juan

Chapter 4   Lake Cocibolca

Lake Cocibolca is huge, 8,264 square kilometres in area, 65 kilometres wide and 160 kilometres long, it is fed by numerous rivers from Nicaragua and Costa Rica, the water eventually draining from the lake to the Atlantic through the Rio San Juan. Essentially a flood plain, the lake lies 31 metres above sea level and although it is relatively shallow, only about 20 metres deep, south-east of Omotepe there are spots where 60 metres have been recorded. And, near San Carlos, a deep mythical emerald mine that is patrolled by sharks. About 1529 Gonzalo Fernandez de Oviedo mentioned in his writings that Lake Cocibolca had many islands covered with forest as well as small islands and rocks between which rose abundant fish. The main islands are Las Isletas near Granada, Zapatera and Omotepe islands in the middle of the lake and the Solentiname group near the southeast corner.

Once the land bridge between the North and South Americas was finally established the water access between the Pacific and the Atlantic was gone, the lake was formed and the fish were trapped. The shark of Lake Cocibolca has long been a biological curiosity along with the 700 pound sawfish, sardines and the gaspar. Gradually the lake became less saline and the fish adapted. Well, that was the story. What is now known is that, when the lakes were formed by the accumulation of fresh water in the Nicaragua Tectonic Depression, the fish, including the bull shark *Carcharhinus leucas*, and the tarpon, had simply migrated up the river from the Atlantic into the lake where they adjusted to the salinity changes, and there they stayed. Even that story had to be adapted after it was discovered that sharks tagged in the lake in the late 1960s, moved freely from ocean to lake. The bull shark is a formidable animal and its speed and power legendary. Lake to ocean can take less than six days and one tagged shark made it to Sicily.

The first shark factory was built in the 1950s and the fins were sold to Chinese traders in Bluefields on the Caribbean coast. Later, a factory was built in Granada by the then president, Somoza, that employed 50 fishermen. Tens of thousands of sharks were slaughtered annually for their fins, skin and oil but by the end of the 1970s catches were dropping and where a shark fisherman would catch one fish a day, it then became one every couple of weeks until none were caught. As soon as the Sandanistas were in power the Granada shark processing plant was closed, shark fishing made illegal and huge fines enforced. Today, it is very rare to find a shark in the lake but there are signs that they are slowly returning.

The sardines thrive as does the guapote, a cichlid, but both are being fished indiscriminately and their stocks too, are dropping.

Getting to the Rio San Juan is not that easy and we wanted to take the canoe around the lake, keeping close to the bank, until we got to the river, stopping at various islands and towns on the way. Everyone we spoke to told us not to risk it. The lake can be deceitfully tranquil, storms suddenly blow up from nowhere and the relatively shallow water becomes very rough, very quickly, and ships have sunk, as adventurers, conquistadors and ferry companies can testify. For some time it was thought that the lake was tidal as the water was pushed towards the west bank by the prevailing wind and, when the wind dropped, the water receded. The east bank of the lake is more sheltered than the west, but our preferred route to the San Juan was around the west bank.

Now, when someone told Joe "you can't do that", it was like a red rag to a bull and his reaction was often, "just because people say you can't do it, doesn't always mean that you can't". We needed to take the canoe and engine for a run as they had not been in the water since Texas, try out the new seats and perhaps, do a bit of fishing. But the real reason was to see how the canoe would perform in the lake and just exactly what the conditions were like. We took the canoe down to the lake and put it in the water near the isletas next to our favourite bar and guapote restaurant, the amazing eating fish with more flesh than you can imagine and served with bones removed and a tomato, onion and garlic sauce. Anything left over went to feed the house crocodile, a big beast, thankfully but sadly kept in a largish concrete cage.

After lunch we puttered around the islands, the little engine buzzing away and the chairs wonderfully comfortable; a great success.

The basalt rocks of the isletas, thrown out by the exploding Mombacho, are today covered with vegetation. No matter whether it is a larger islands or just a cluster of rocks, wherever a plant can find a foothold, there it will grow. There are palms, vines, exotic flowers, mangoes, papayas, bananas and a wide variety of forest trees. Amongst all this vegetation lives a remarkable array of birds. Oropendulas with their gurgling calls and distinctive brown and yellow plumage flash amongst the trees. Their pendulous nests, about three feet in length sway from branches that overhang the water. There are herons and kingfishers, jacanas and cormorants, birds that were to become very familiar to us over the following days.

Many of the isletas now have luxury holiday homes built on them by foreigners and wealthy Nicaraguans, some of them dating from the days of the piñata, the land free for all at the end of the Sandanista/Contra war. But the next island may be home to some of the poorest Granadanians, living in wooden shacks with a few chickens, ducks and maybe a pig or two, keeping a precarious grip on their world.

The canoe performed well as we nosed around the islands, and Joe decided to take it past one of the outer islands and into the lake. Here, there was little protection from the easterly prevailing wind and even on a calm day such as this, there were ripples. The canoe puttered through these but a couple of wavelets later it was quite clear that the canoe just could not cope. Water sprayed into the boat, the bow jumped when headed into the wavelets (nobody could possibly call them waves) and it was completely unstable when they came broadside on. We retreated into calm waters and back to the bar.

We were well satisfied with the canoe's performance but all thoughts of getting to the Rio San Juan via the lake had disappeared. We gazed over the water and watched a heron fishing. It stood on both legs with one shimmying in the mud, its head and beak making sudden darts to catch whatever it had scared. A woman rowed a heavy wooden canoe over to the dock, first one oar pulled through the water, then the other, the Nicaraguan shuffle Joe called it. Flocks of egrets flew over-head, their omo white feathers caught the evening light and shone against the darkening sky. They paused on a rock before taking off again to settle in a tree where after jockeying precariously for position they roost for the night, the tree seemed from a distance as though covered with large white cotton balls.

Getting to the San Juan was now a choice of taking the twice weekly, overnight, ferry from Granada to San Carlos, the plane or driving. The ferryboat is reminiscent of the African Queen and takes about 15 hours with little in the way of comfort, certainly no cabins. The aeroplane was completely out of the question. The last option was to drive.

"Well", Joe complained, "I hate to admit it but everyone was right, we certainly can't take the canoe down the lake, it will have to be that god-awful road".

Chapter 5   Granada to San Carlos

What to take, and what not to take, gave rise to animated discussions. Oars, anchor, spare propeller, a few tools and fuel cans, were must haves; as were drinking water, sunscreen and insect repellent. Fishing rods, umbrellas, machete and torches were high on Joe's list; notebook, pens, bird book and binoculars essential for me. Most things were packed in a watertight box that would fit in the centre of the canoe, with the squashy bags of clothes stuffed around it. There was an impressive amount of stuff. We put a foam mattress on top of the car, more to protect the car than the canoe, lifted the canoe on top and strapped it down tightly to withstand the trip to San Carlos.

The road grazes around the north and east of Lake Cocibolca so from Granada, you drive to the lake turn left and just keep going. When we left it was one of those blue sky, white fluffy clouds days; a blue haze veiled the hills on the far side of the lake where we were headed and the sun glinted off the ripples. The lake is a popular place and Nicaraguans are great party people and even in the mid 1800s:

> '…the shore was crowded with bathers, and washerwomen and idlers'.

> 'With horses mingling amongst the people.'

Today the lake is still a favourite place and the bathers and washerwomen, idlers and horses are all still there, though Granada itself has grown from 15,000 people to 111,000. Today Granadanians arrive at the lake in their pick-up's, horses and carts and possibly even an ox cart or two, all

Rio San Juan

laden with plastic chairs, hammocks and awnings, food and drink including plenty of Flor de Cana rum and the most enormous bottles of cola. Vendors set up their stalls frying or grilling chicken and meat served on banana leaf plates with copious amounts of the local cole slaw, fried platano, rice and beans. Always eaten with fingers there is absolutely nothing to wash up. Women, men and children play in the water; rarely bothering to change clothes they just walk straight into the shallow water; trousers, skirts, dresses, blouses, whatever they are wearing.

Mark Twain on his visit in 1866 was engaged by a similar scene in Nicaragua and incomparably described the local maidens, about whom:

'…the males of their group were not oblivious…about every two hundred yards throughout the journey…..they are singularly full in the bust…They are virtuous according to their lights….but I guess their lights are a little dim.'

And of two particular girls:

'…such liquid languishing eyes! such pouting lips! such glossy,
luxuriant hair! such ravishing, incendiary expressions! such grace! such voluptuous forms! such precious little drapery about them!'

He might be glad to know that not much has changed!

We drove on east through one of Nicaragua's cultural mixes. Wooden shacks roofed with tin or palm or patched with plastic bags and planks of wood; chickens and fat, comfortable pigs and nosy piglets, rootling around outside and sometime inside too. Some of the pigs had sticks tied around their necks looking like medieval torture instruments but the sticks simply there to keep the pigs out of the precious vegetable gardens. The houses, many with earth floors inside, are surrounded by flattened bare earth to keep the snakes at bay but no matter how poor, there were flowers; hibiscus, bougainvillea, cannas and heliconias that made every house cheerful. Women and children cleaned and swept their earth patios, or sprayed them with water to keep the dust down whilst cooking the inevitable rice and beans. A crowd had gathered at the communal laundry with its concrete sinks and water well as clothes washing with its never-ending pile is a social event. Children pulled up buckets of water, giggling and squealing as most of the water was tipped over each other. The barbed wire fences were decorated with drying laundry and there is clearly a skill to this as everything from socks to sheets were impaled and when the wind blows they strain against the wire. The only time that I had tried this I ended up with two substantial holes in one of Joe's shirts. A cheery wave with soapy hand and literally next door, we passed a million dollar house with manicured and exotic gardens, a huge aviary and a couple of exquisite horses, ready saddled, waiting in the shade. $60,000 cars in the garage and a $150,000 boat waiting to be launched. The staff house far better than anything the campesinos could ever hope to have. The years of war have left the poor, poorer, the country more or less destitute and the rich, richer.

The driving was slow, not just because of the state of the road, which was dirt or mud and full of ruts and holes, but also because of the animals, which were everywhere.

Rio San Juan

Chickens and pigs and half-starved dogs lay listlessly on the road. Horses grazed along the verges and beautiful huge golden oxen slowly pulled carts whilst a family or two of cattle would stroll along, en-route to some new grazing place. All had to be carefully negotiated whilst we received stares and waves as we passed with our shiny canoe.

We passed a school painted in the blue and white national colours, a Nicaraguan flag flying. Next door was a bar decorated with election slogans and colourful beer advertisements and then, a convent with high walls, totally detached from the world around it.

Driving away from the township we were soon in farmland with rich soil and plenty of water. Ranches with healthy cattle and dairy cows and high-stepping horses ridden to show off horsemanship skills during the horse parades. There were cowboys wearing jeans, chaps, hats and skilfully made boots from towns in the north and leather thongs swung from their fancy saddles. The skills of the rodeo are, for them, just everyday work. Rice and beans, corn, and sugarcane were growing in the fields. Nicaragua must be one of the highest consumers of sugar in the world but at least some of the cane goes to make the wonderful Flor de Caña rums. There were stands of platanos and bananas, mango, coconut and cashew trees and other fruits that were a complete mystery to us but which confirmed Nicaragua as the country of a thousand fruits.

In 1635 an English Dominican Friar, Thomas Gage, was also travelling around the lake. He had been in Mexico and Guatemala for the last ten years and had become disenchanted with the Catholic interpretation of Christianity and wanted to return to England. He could not get any help from the Church so, as he had become relatively wealthy, he decided to run away and make his own way home. He decided to go south, to Nicaragua, as there he would be less likely to run into any people that he knew and ships were fairly regular. Once in Nicaragua he wrote:

'…..from hence to Granada I observed nothing but the plainness and pleasantness of the way, which with the fruits and fertility of all things may well make Nicaragua the Paradise of America.'

He was making his way by mule, following, like us, the shore of Lake Nicaragua when he describes the following encounter.

'The second day after we set out we were much affrighted with a huge and monstrous cayman or crocodile, which, having come out of the lake (which we passed by), and lying across a puddle of water bathing himself, and waiting for some prey, as we perceived after, when we, not knowing well at the first, but thinking that it had been some tree that was felled or fallen, passed close by it; when on a sudden we knew the scales of the cayman, and saw the monster stir and move, and set himself against us; wherewith we made haste from him, but he thinking to have made some of us his greedy prey, ran after us, which when we perceived, and that he was like to overtake us, we were much troubled, until one of the Spaniards (who knew better the nature and quality of that beast than the rest) called upon us to turn to one side out of the way, and to ride on straight for a while, and then to turn to another side, and so to circumflex our way, which advice without doubt saved mine or some of the others' lives, for thus we wearied that mighty monster and escaped from him….'.

Rio San Juan

Today, Caimans can be found throughout the lake and river system, notably in the Rio Papaturo near the southern end of the lake, close to the border with Costa Rica, where a research centre has a breeding programme. The crocodile is much less common but may be encountered near the mouth of the river but they will probably never be seen again in the numbers and sizes, some over four metres long, described by early travellers. The cloud of vultures we saw circling ahead on the road, turned out to be concerned with nothing more exotic than dead dog. Uncared for, the dogs are often skinny and disease ridden, but any suggestion that perhaps they would be better off destroyed is met with horror.

A black heavy-billed ani sat on a fence whilst others pecked around the fence posts for insects. Grackles picked ticks off the hides of cattle whilst white egrets fed on insects flushed out by their hoofs. A long thin brown snake sped across the road. We knew that there were plenty of snakes around, some extremely dangerous, but this was one of only two we saw on our whole trip. Yellow-breasted flycatchers perched, and occasionally swooped for some unseen prey. At our house in Granada, they flew down for the ripe, bright red, bird chillies that are so fantastically hot it seems quite strange that they can eat them with such relish. Vines and other plants grew unattended and intertwined and everywhere there were butterflies, fantasies of colour and pattern. Most were flitting around but others were settled in dense groups on the ground by the side of the road where they had been attracted by the crystals of drying urine from cattle and horses. We must have hit butterfly season as there were so many and every day they brightened our trip.

We passed a cemetery, simple graves with wooden crosses, some with photographs of the deceased and many decorated with, slightly faded, plastic flowers left from the celebration of The Day of the Dead. Funerals are big and vary from the grand black carriage horses of Granada draped with white or black net, that pull an elaborately carved black wooden hearse covered with wreathes and carrying the coffin, to the cathedral and then on to the cemetery to a country funeral that we came upon one day. The coffin was hoisted high on the shoulders of six friends or family and was, literally, danced to the cemetery, the whole village following. The coffin bobbed up and down as it was lifted high above the heads of the carriers and then brought head down, almost to touch the ground, and wove its way from side to side along the road all to the accompaniment of the local band. Part of the exuberance was quickly apparent by the alcoholic fumes accompanying the mourners; but they made it and laid their friend to rest with celebration.

We kept the lake on our right hand side; a gentle shoreline of grass and patches of reeds, horses grazing, drinking and splashing in the shallows. This stretch of the lake, close to Granada, with its calm waters and easy access to the town was to be of some importance in later events concerning the city. Boats could easily pull up at night and discharge men who could then walk into the city.

Soon we reached the Tipitapa river, which we had to cross by a rather broken down car ferry. The last time we tried to do this the ferry was completely out of commission and we had had to return to Granada to take a much longer, circuitous route, to get to our destination. It was with relief that we found it operating and cautiously drove on, together with an ancient blue and white cattle truck and a motorbike, all of us parking under a bright yellow Victoria beer awning. It was soon apparent that all was not well with the ferry engine and that the boat was being hauled over the river by hand, all able-bodied people, including Joe, were out helping to pull on the cable. A herd of horses crossed the river beside us and swam through the water, negotiating the floating clumps of water hyacinth and lake cabbage. They seemed quite anxious when swimming but the ease with which they climbed the far bank made us think that it was probably a daily trip and the crocodiles were long gone. Behind the ferry we pulled a brand-new dug-out canoe painted bright blue that skittered from one side of the boat to the other. We wondered if it was the lifeboat.

"Nice boat." Remarked Joe.

The destination of the horses soon became clear when we passed a hacienda that had seen better days but was still beautiful with its tiled roof, wooden columns and verandas. Rice meadows stretched before us and here were feeding the flocks of egrets that had accompanied us. Long-legged tractors paddled through the fields and though much of the farm equipment was modern, nearly every farm had an old Russian tractor sitting on a small hill. Joe said that they were notorious for not starting and that the only way to get them going was by letting them roll down a slope. So, perched on their hills where they had been parked after their last trip was where they had stayed.

Until this point the road had just been bad, now it was terrible. Horses and ox carts were the main means of transport and everyone seemed to ride, mothers with babies, children, the grandparents and, of course, the cowboys. The oxen were the most beautiful, calm animals with huge eyes and lengthy lashes and long ears. They were used for carting everything and in many places were still the most reliable haulage system, one pair coming to our rescue one day when we got stuck in a riverbed.

Sadly, these beautiful animals too might be part of Nicaragua's history but while much of the valuable, productive land for small farmers is full of stones spewed from volcanoes, the ox plough may survive for a bit longer yet.

Our erratic course, the car with the canoe on top slipping and sliding was the source of much amusement, laughter and many giggles for the children who ran alongside us, some even pausing in a baseball game, the national passion, to watch us pass. Every weekend there are baseball matches, even in the depths of the country where horses line up patiently waiting for the game to end side by side with 4x4 wheel drive vehicles. Better baseball than cockfighting, also a national sport, with its small arenas, bloody birds and noisy, gesticulating, betting crowd.

We had been following the road alongside a river and looking for a bridge to cross it but the road was getting worse and worse and eventually petered out completely. We had left our map at home. Well, we knew the way didn't we? This, however, turned out to be a mistake and spotting a Coca Cola van, we asked for directions. San Carlos was a complete mystery to the driver but, eventually, we were able to describe the general direction in which we wanted to go and were told to: "Just drive over the river". We drove to the edge and looked suspiciously at the water. A couple of cowboys on horses plunged in and, hoping that they were taking the shallow route, we followed them. The Range Rover jerked over a couple of rocks and splashed through; no problem!

At the next village we found a Pepsi Cola van the driver of which confirmed our route but warned us that the road was not good, that we should do what he did and go via Granada! He was quite right that that road was better, just 100 kilometres longer, and as we were already well on our way around the lake we were not inclined to turn around and start again. He was also right about the road ahead, it was a series of deep, slippery, ruts that had to be carefully negotiated so that we did not end up sitting in the ditch or perched on top of a ridge.

Just when you thought that you really were in the middle of nowhere, suddenly there was a school, a church, then houses and we were onto the smooth, straight, main road with its supermarkets, bars, restaurants, tyre mending shops, churches and auto-hotels, these a way of getting around the strict Catholic marriage codes. The rooms are let out by the hour or however long you want and each room has an en-suite garage with a huge curtain swished behind the vehicle to hide it and its number plate, and protect the owner from his or her indiscretion.

A few miles on and the good road veered off to Rama and Bluefields on the Atlantic and we were left with a corrugated, tarmac stressed road for 130 kilometres that would take about six hours of very unpleasant driving.

It was the rainy season and a time of plenty for the animals with grass up to their shoulders. We passed extensive platano plantations, a calorie packed fruit loaded with minerals that is eaten at most meals. It is usually roasted or fried, when it is very good, but sometimes it is just boiled when it is an acquired taste and should probably be avoided at all costs.

Birds were everywhere, green parrots as described by Belt:

'…. fly over in screaming flocks'.

There were black tanagers with red rumps that flashed amongst the roadside foliage, and grackles. The grackles are large black birds with a long tail that the males fold up into a V shape. The great-tailed or Mexican grackle is a widespread species that used to live in mangroves and marshes, estuaries and mud flats (wet, soggy places) but has now spread into open farmland, villages, towns, gardens and parks where they are often seen in a courtship display, facing each other their necks and beaks stretched straight up and pointed towards the sky. Its smaller relative, the Nicaraguan grackle, still manages to hold its own with its bossy relative.

We rumbled and lurched down the road, glad that we had the canoe cushioned on its mattress, and drove into an area of marsh and rice farms. The rice production is extraordinary and from one huge rice farm on the opposite side of the lake we had seen three crops harvested in one year.

A few vehicles passed us, going in the opposite direction, one, a truck carrying three enormous tree trunks that had come from Sábalos down the San Juan. Then, in front of us, two vans were parked. These turned out to be the travelling supermarket. The first had bread, cakes, vegetables and fruit, rice and beans, sugar and flour and the non-perishable essentials. The second, was piled high with a rainbow of plastic; chairs stacked together and hung on the sides, bowls, buckets, containers of every size, brushes and mops, plastic sheeting for roof leaks, and much more. Business was brisk!

The drive had taken longer than we had anticipated so we decided not to try to get to San Carlos that evening and arrive in the dark. On a previous trip we had had to spend two nights in San Carlos and, on arrival, had wondered why everyone had heavy black plastic sheeting over their windows and doors. It looked like a war-time black-out. The enemy, it turned out, were lake flies. We were familiar with lake flies, having spent some time working at a fishing lodge on Lake Victoria in Africa. There we would see them as clouds over the lake and sometimes they would drift to land when they could be a real problem. At their worst, they were everywhere, day and night they were in your food, in your drinks, in your hair and your nostrils. But, after a day or two they would move off elsewhere. In San Carlos it was a different story. The flies were much bigger, emerged at sunset and homed-in on any light. Every evening the black sheeting was securely fastened around windows and over doors, arranged like the double doors in a photographic dark room. Walking down the street to the restaurant, a handkerchief firmly secured around your mouth, a flashlight pointing at the street for holes and loose cobbles (there is no street lighting), you walked as fast as you could. On reaching the restaurant the curtain was pulled back briefly, you shimmied around the edge after which it was, again, firmly tied back. You shook off the flies and opened the second door for supper. A blast of music greeted you along with mouth-watering smells of cooking fish and meat.

Next morning the dead flies were swept up into heaps while the live ones had disappeared until the evening. Even in the 1850s they were a nuisance and it was recorded that 'the gnats' were swept up by the bucket load from ships' decks before being dumped into the river. On enquiring about them we were told that they were only around for a short time of the year and noone had any idea about their habits, where they bred or what happened to them for the rest of the year.

Rather than face the flies again on this trip, we branched off to San Miguelito, a small town on the bank of Lake Cociboloca that does have a hotel and a restaurant.

We had our first experience here of some of the NGO's non-governmental organisations, that have flocked to this part of Nicaragua. It was actually quite difficult to find out exactly what they are all doing and when I did ask one group in another part of the country, and was told that they had been building churches, I was appalled. The people can build churches themselves but they already have thousands and you do not need much in the way of a building in this climate anyway. What about water and sewage systems, medical care, education, birth control? We later came across a church with an ecological theme in the town. It didn't look as though it had many followers and perhaps ecological soul saving was before its time.

We parked the car outside the hotel and a group of grubby, cheerful, children surrounded it and jumped up to touch the canoe and asked us where we were going. They had formed themselves into a band and were beating old coco cola bottles with sticks, wearing random second-hand t-shirts, one commemorating a Brown family reunion!

The hotel was next to the jetty where the Granada to San Carlos ferry stops each trip. This was a ferry day, or rather, night, as it arrived around 3.00 am. The foyer of the hotel was cluttered with half a dozen people, one a huge woman squeezed into a rocking chair, luggage was piled around including a large number of buckets that we later discovered held cheese. San Miguelito cheese is one of the better Nicaraguan cheeses, if you like the soft variety, and is very good in a tortilla and microwaved for a few seconds, especially with avocado.

We settled ourselves into a simple but clean room with a huge veranda that looked out over the lake. Out came the rejuvenating rum and coke and we gazed through the evening light at the Solentiname islands in the distance and the peaks of Omotepe to the west, whilst a tiny buff-coloured house wren busily pecked at insects in cracks and crannies around the veranda for a late night snack.

" I would really like to go to Solentiname one day and see if they are still painting pictures there." I murmured.

A really good guapote supper in the only local restaurant, music and entertainment provided by a manic tame parrot in a tree, and then, home to bed. Three o'clock in the morning and we were awakened by a loud ships hooter. The boat had arrived and a dozen or so people were getting on, including the huge lady downstairs who had been brought to her feet by people holding onto both arms and pulling hard as she rocked forward and swayed, happily, up. All the luggage and cheese had been packed away. Vendors were out with hammocks to hang on the deck and plastic sheeting to tie over the hammock to keep one dry and warm, chicken, sweet pastries, sugary fruit drinks, tortillas, cheese and various snacks. It is not surprising to see why Nicaragua has a weight problem. "Café caliente" is being loudly hawked.

"Don't try it", Joe tells me, "I've done that, it's cold!"

Ten minutes later the ferry left and everything had disappeared.

We left San Miguelito early, the ferry had disturbed our night and we were ready to leave before the sun was up. A cheerful woman in her flowered nightgown was happy to make us a cup of coffee, which we drank together with a pastry, her small daughter having been dispatched, at a run, to buy them at the local bakery. The drive to San Carlos took two and half uneventful hours. As we reached the town we passed a timber yard with huge logs stacked high, a sawmill and large driers for the cut wood. Cut in the forests near Sábalos on the Rio San Juan, these are some of the last trees that can legally come from there. We had seen the price of wood soar whilst we had been in Nicaragua and where we used to buy cedro real (the hard cedar) for 20 cents for 1 inch square and 1 vara (33 inches) long, less than three years later it was double that.

We headed straight for the bus station in San Carlos as this was where we would get a proper breakfast. A series of small restaurants serve meals all day and night, and pretty girls in immaculate make-up, tight-fitting jeans and lycra tops, tout for business for their restaurant. Fending off the hawkers with their watches and sunglasses, pirated cds, naturally made local products, and the inevitable shoe-shine boys, we dined on unlimited coffee, beans and rice, eggs, fried hard cheese and platano and were now prepared for anything! We must have arrived on some kind of festival day as a band was playing and a twirly lady (our name) dancing. Models of woman about ten feet tall with long hair and dressed in long full skirts are hoisted onto a man's shoulders and with the skirt almost touching the ground he twirls around to the music, first one way, then the other, long hair and arms circling around the body of the mannequin. Fireworks were let off, the louder the better and music blared from every corner, one shop with huge speakers set up outside to, supposedly attract customers, the noise was ear-splitting.

The girl at the café, the hostess, sat down to chat with us while we were eating and asked where we were going with the canoe.

"San Juan del Norte"

. "Oh you are going to Costa Rica!" She cheerfully said

This rather bemused us but later we knew what she meant.

"Are you going to be alright over the rapids, your canoe looks very small?" She asked, concerned.

Personally, I thought that she might be right to ask but Joe assured her that there would be no problem. We paid, the woman owner being ushered over to take the money that disappeared rapidly into one of the many pockets of her frilly, tiered apron that doubled as a handbag.

San Carlos is not a town that you choose to visit. It is decaying, has terrible streets and is dirty. It is unfortunate that such an unattractive place is the gateway to some of the most wondrous places in Nicaragua. The town exists because of its situation, at the head of the Rio San Juan. All the boats that go up and down the river and across the lake come and go from here. Things are looking up for the town though as roads are being repaired and the main road, the one that we had just driven along, is scheduled for rebuilding and as most of the supplies for the town have to come down this road, it should make an enormous difference to the local population. As tourism becomes more important, an easier way to reach San Carlos, the lake, the islands and the river will be welcomed.

We parked the car by a small hotel where we knew that it would be safe to leave it and from where we could launch the canoe. A couple of wooden shacks were built up on stilts, chickens and pigs strolling around underneath, ducks and geese in and around the water and a few guinea fowl scratched in the dust. The kitchen was outside and a woman tended a small wood fire, cooking beans. A wooden walkway led from the car park to a small dock and almost as soon as we had driven in a group of three men came towards us, an older man, a younger man and a boy, all clearly related. Before we had said more than a few words to them, the canoe was off the car, the box and our bags, out. When we turned around again, they were all down on the dock and the canoe in the water. Joe went to oversee the packing. How on earth could we possibly have so much gear? There were mounds of things. Did we really need all those ropes? Joe was completely unperturbed and amazingly everything was squirreled away somewhere, two tame parrots loudly directed the operations from the lower branches of an overhanging mango tree. The box was firmly lodged in the middle of the canoe and bags of clothes, wrapped in thick plastic bags, stuffed in on each side (after eight weeks with both of us and a tent on one Vespa, you learn to pack small, but that is another story). Oars and anchor were put where they would be easily accessible, as was a half coca-cola bottle for bailing.   My small bag with sunscreen, mosquito spray, binoculars, notebook and pen, water and granola bars for lunch, rainwear, shirt and spare hat were tucked under my seat in the front.

"OK let's go!"

Chapter 6   Early Explorers

The European exploration of Central America was primarily concerned with finding a route across the land bridge that separated the two great oceans, the Pacific and the Atlantic. Since Balboa's expedition of 1513 and the discovery of the Pacific Ocean from Panama, it had been found that, in some places, the land strip between the oceans was only 80 kilometres. There was much enthusiasm about a road, or even a canal, across this piece of land but what nagged at people was the thought that there was a natural waterway joining the two oceans. The coasts of the whole of Central America were being searched for river outlets and estuaries. Spain was in the forefront of the search with huge rewards of fame and fortune should such a waterway be found. In 1519 the Pacific coast from Panama to N. Nicaragua was searched and no outlet found. In 1521 Gil Gonzáles Dávila left from Panama to explore north along the Atlantic but instead of going all the way by boat, he took a land route, following the coast. At some point he headed inland and, from the top of a hill, spread out before him was a huge sheet of water. For a while he thought that it might be the Pacific but, on tasting it, the water was sweet and he declared it the Mar Dulce, the Freshwater Sea, and remarked that he did not know of any body of freshwater so extensive in Europe. He walked his horse into the water and raised the flag of Castilla and in a loud voice, with sword unsheathed, took possession of Lake Cocibolca in the name of the sovereign of Spain. He ended the ceremony by drinking some of the water of the lake from his helmet.

At that time, as many as two million people may have lived around the shore of the lake. Sixteen years later, less than one quarter remained. Diseases had destroyed, many were killed in combat, others had been taken into slavery and the rest had fled.

Gonzáles knew that the water from this lake had to go somewhere, it had to spill into a river and then down to a sea. He desperately sought information from his local Nicarao Indian guides as, besides his thirst for exploration and discovery, there was fame and fortune to think of. The Indians were divided into numerous tribes, each governed by "caiques" or chiefs, sometimes by councils, and every tribe member was readily identified by tattoo marks. At one meeting with the great Indian chief, Nicoya, Gonzáles was offered:

'...14 thousand pieces of eight in gold, 13 carats fine and six idols of the same metal each a span long'.

In return, Gonzáles gave him some Spanish toys and baptised him and all his subjects, some six thousand in total. Gold was not the main thrust of his trip but it was not something to be ignored. The Indians knew all about gold and were skilled smiths. Gonzáles went on to talk with Chief Nicaragua and was given yet more presents:

'...25 thousand gold pieces of eight and many garments and plumes of feathers'.

In return, 9,000 were baptised. When Gonzáles pressed the chief about how and where they got the gold, and whether the lake had any access to the sea, Nicaragua feigned complete ignorance (as did Gonzáles's guides) and denied all knowledge of any river, even though it is likely that they and their ancestors had been using it for many, many, years particularly as the chief source of the gold was not Nicaragua but Costa Rica, Mexico and Panama.

Eventually, news that a river did exist leaked out and, in 1522 Gonzáles at last found the outlet of the river from the lake.

The town of San Carlos was later founded on the lake on a strategically placed small peninsula that had a convenient hill from where there were views across the mouths of both the Rio San Juan and the Rio Frio and along the lake. It was the gateway to the San Juan and of the utmost strategic importance.

Once news leaked out that Gonzáles had found an outlet to a river that he was convinced led to the Atlantic, the race was on. Gonzáles had run out of resources to explore the river himself and, as the Indians were proving less than cooperative, he returned to Spain and there tried to get another expedition together to go and conquer and settle the country. But, Pedrarias D'Avila, who in 1522 was governing the region, sent the conquistador Francisco Hernández de Córdoba to Nicaragua and Hernán Cortéz too, was exploring in the area.

These three were now racing for exploration, fame and fortune. Gonzáles had raised an army and was fighting against Córdoba and the country around them was in turmoil. Their excesses all stemmed from personal jealousy and rivalry that took very little notice of the directives and orders that came from Spain. Hernández de Córdoba was the eventual winner and he went on to found Granada on the northern bank of Lake Cocibolca alongside an existing Chorotega community and later, founded the settlement of León.

In 1525 he sent his captain, Ruy Diaz, to find the river outlet from the lake, and explore the river. Diaz was the first foreigner to travel on the river and although, on his first expedition, his ship was only able to get as far as the first rapids, he reached the second set on his following trip.

Pascual de Andagoya, writing of Nicaragua at that time describes:

'…a country populous and fertile, yielding supplies of maize and many fowls of the country, and certain small dogs which they also eat, and many deer and fish. This is a land of abundance of good fruit and of honey and wax, wherewith all the neighbouring countries are supplied.'

Of the women:

'They had many beautiful women. The men were so much under subjection that if they make their wives angry they were turned out of doors and the wives even raised their hands against them.'

But all this changed with the power of the Spaniards and the women were soon brought to heel to do most of the labour.

D'Avila was a ruthless commander and when Córdoba attempted to become the Governor of Nicaragua, D'Avila had him beheaded and he himself took on the position, moved to León and died at the remarkably old age of 87. Nicaragua remained a Spanish possession for the next 300 years.

Meanwhile, exploration had continued elsewhere and Hernán Cortéz landed in Mexico in 1519 and discovered an Aztec empire. Montezuma was in charge but, eventually, his own people turned against him and he was stoned to death and New Spain founded. Two years later, Cortéz was beginning to build Mexico City.

Pizarro left Spain for Peru in 1532 and found an Inca civilization. He eventually conquered and ten years later, Spain controlled most of South and Central America. Pizarro also left what is probably the first map of Nicaragua, a most beautifully illustrated chart drawn on sheepskin that shows both Granada and León and is thought to date from around 1540.

Both Cortéz and Pizarro found huge quantities of gold and silver including the Potosi silver mine, now in Bolivia. A mountain of silver 15,381 feet high producing, with imported gold, riches worth about $774 million.

And Spain was keeping its hold on it all.

Chapter 7   San Carlos to Sábalos

The sky was dark but tinged with purple, a sure sign of rain. The lake was calm, no wind and the sky would, we hoped, clear. Joe confidently stepped into the canoe, settled himself into a chair and commanded me to get aboard.

"But, don't rock the canoe."

I stepped gingerly in, sat down and stowed my bag, so far so good. I grabbed a paddle and pushed off from the bank whilst Joe tried to start the engine. My paddling experience was non-existent and we were headed straight for one of the local women, standing thigh high in water, scrubbing away, washing clothes in her personal concrete washing sink set in the lake. The engine had not started and seeing my complete incompetence, Joe took over oar steering and headed us back towards the lake.

"Just keep it straight."

This time we headed directly for the main dock in town and the passenger ferry. The current, curved around the bank and was carrying us towards the mouth of the river (and the dock) when, with some relief, the engine started. This was the only time on the entire trip that it was reluctant to start on the first attempt.

People waved as we passed by the docks and piers where boats come and go from Granada, Papatura, Solentiname, Los Chiles, San Juan del Norte and all stops on the river as our engine made us sound like a freight train rather a tiny silver canoe. Except for the Granada ferry, the boats were lanchas, about 10 varas long with an awning on top to keep sun and rain at bay and they carried everything and anything. There were separate docks for big freight and it was here that the tree trunks we had seen on the road and at the sawmill were unloaded.

Rio San Juan

The real adventure had begun, we were off down the Rio San Juan.

We were now out of the lake and really on the river and the canoe was doing well, the engine pushed us along, albeit with a current flowing with us, at about four kilometres an hour very satisfactorily. We sorted ourselves out in the canoe, moved a few things around to get it as stable as possible, tossed the sunscreen and drinking water between us and I, just sat back and enjoyed the scenery.

Immediately past San Carlos there were shacks on the edge of town and some richer houses with manicured gardens but these soon gave way to dense vegetation on both sides of the river with cattle ranches behind. Our leeboard was only a few inches above the water so it was quite impossible to see far through the plants on either side of the river; the ranches could have extended for 100 metres or a

100 kilometres for all we could see. The river was a wide shining ribbon that curved and cut through the vegetation; the clouds had not dispersed and the sky was slate grey. Flying flocks of white egrets, brightly lit by sunlight looked almost ghost-like against the gloomy sky. But the clouds were moving and they were soon gone and the sun was radiant. Pushed by the water current, water hyacinths clogged the banks and amongst them were dugout canoes with men fishing. Their skin naturally dark but bronzed by the sun they were muscled by a life of manual labour.

The bank-side vegetation was a complete mixture but dominated by cane, this, or a similar variety, was used in the ceilings of all the colonial houses in Granada. There were tall leaved *Heliconias* with spiky red and yellow 'bird' flowers and amongst them butterflies fluttered, the whole country seemed to have exploded with them. Velvet black scarlet rumped tanagers flashed red whilst yellow flycatchers twisted in the air for delicacies. The water lilies with their yellow and white flowers amongst the purple spikes of water hyacinths were like an embroidered oriental carpet. Delicate dragonflies balanced on leaves and dodged the jacanas. With their brown plumage with yellow underwings that flashed in flight, a flap, flap, flap, glide, the jacanas are some of the most attractive birds on the river. They hold their wings high and together over their backs on alighting and bob amongst the hyacinths or walk on the lily pads, their long toes spreading their weight to not sink the pad. The female defends her territory, and her entourage of maybe three or four male birds and although each male builds its own nest, she may give them some help and encouragement. She mates with each bird, lays eggs in each nest and leaves the males to incubate them. On hatching, it is, again, the males that primarily watch over and protect the chicks.

Herons were lined up along the river-bank, irrespective of species each had its own stretch of bank, one bird more or less equidistant from the other.

We passed a crowd of cormorants collectively feeding on the river, the birds all bunched together forced fish into the shallows where they were easy prey; but our engine disturbed them and one by one they raised their wings, slowly became airborne and with necks stretched out skimmed across the river to land further away to repeat the process all over again.

There was a fruit farm on the south bank with rows of citrus trees ranked by age. Nicaragua used to be the breadbasket of Central America but one result of its past conflict was that farmland was lost and markets with it.

We passed wooden houses with open verandas and spaces for windows. Built on stilts to protect against rising waters, some were no better than shacks but another group of buildings with extensive docks and manicured lawns and flowers declared itself a research station, the only place we passed with "keep out, private" signs.

At last, the sun came out and we continued downstream aided by the current. We passed dugouts going upstream, hugging the bank where the current was less strong, everybody on board paddling, no matter the age or sex, all helped to nudge their canoe forward. It could take three times as long to go upstream than down. Some of the canoes had only a couple of inches of wood showing above the water, battered and blackened, the wood silky smooth where it had been handled for tens of years they will be kept and used until, eventually, they disintegrate. The river was now flowing faster and after an hour and ten minutes, our engine puttered, then died. We were out of fuel and had to transfer some from our spare cans. Now that we knew how long the tank would last we had a very convenient way of keeping track of time and this became our measure of the river. We drifted down with the current, no engine, and no noise. We took the opportunity for a drink of water and an application of more sunscreen. For the first time we could hear the noises of the river, the water was calm, almost silent, with barely a ripple but we could hear the birds in the trees. We just enjoyed the tranquility.

"We can't go all the way with no engine, even if we paddled, it would just take too long and we wouldn't get to Sábalos tonight." Joe regretfully commented

We started the engine and continued.

The banks were more forested now and, from our low viewpoint, the farms and ranches seemed to have disappeared. We could see trees, though how far they stretched, we had no idea but in the distance we heard a chainsaw, so the forest may not be much more than just a strip along the riverbank. Later we learnt that there is substantial forest up to the Costa Rica border on the south bank of the river but from there on much has been cleared for farmland. A squadron of 30 or more cormorants flew down the river in a V formation and this first flight was followed by flight after flight. Hundreds of these birds must have passed us and settled in the trees and floated on the water. They roost and breed around the Solentiname islands and Zapote island, which has over 10,000 pairs of nesting birds, the majority of which are cormorants but there are also white egrets, herons and roseate spoonbills. Although we saw the cormorants the whole length of the river these huge congregations along the first kilometres were, perhaps, just commuters.

The river and forested banks were mesmerizing. Palms held feathery heads high in the air whilst others, with dark green shaggy leaves, bent down towards the water. Clumps of fruits and huge clusters of creamy flower heads hummed with insects. Leaves came in every shade of green and every shape, small or huge; creepers and lianas climbed high into the trees while flowers of yellow, blue, red or orange, were blazes of colour amongst the green background. We saw a flash of red wings, parrots shrieking at each other in a fruit-bearing tree. We headed for the bank and pulled in under a tree where we tied the canoe to a convenient branch and got out for a few minutes. We stretched a bit and I congratulated Joe on the chairs, as without them, we would certainly have been aching and probably very fractious.

We glanced into the shallow, clear water near the bank and were amazed by dense schools of small fish. Some were really tiny whilst others were a bit bigger but each size stayed together in its own group. It was like a living fish soup and this, together with the abundance of dragonflies and other insects, answered our questions as to how all the water birds could find enough to eat. No wonder that the birds kept

Rio San Juan

close to shore and an ever-present meal. A cereal bar for each of us, more water to drink and we were off again.

We stayed close to the bank to look at the birds, white egrets, large and small; snowy egrets with their delicate trailing feathers and the magnificent regal great egrets. Pure white, they stretched their necks upwards and then turned their heads 180 degrees so that their beaks pointed down towards the water where they watched, completely still, for any prey. The characteristic darting movement of their head that shoots their beak downwards to spear a fish is only made possible because of special neck vertebrae. Small purple coloured herons, a striped variety and black and white night herons sat hunched amongst the tangled vegetation. Large blue ringed kingfishers were perched on overhanging branches and small iridescent blue pygmy kingfishers flew from branch to branch.

The long neck of an anhinga, a bit like a periscope, slid past. Except for the head and sharply pointed beak the rest of the bird was underwater its feathers spread like a half opened fan. Somehow it took to the air and flew off to the nearest perch to spread its waterlogged wings to dry before it could fish again. Rather odd for a water bird, but we saw the characteristic shape of anhingas with their wings hanging out to dry every day.

The sun was high now and hot, the lowering clouds had dissipated to be replaced by a blue sky and white clouds. The sky and clouds were reflected in the river as was the forest on either side; it was rather like travelling down a tunnel with the water so calm that you couldn't tell top from bottom.

The current brought all kinds of things down the river but, remarkably, practically no rubbish, an odd coca-cola bottle but not much else. What were floating down were plants. Water hyacinths passed, floating along on their bladders of air, their purple flower spikes cheered the scene as did the beautiful cabbage like heads of water lettuce that accompanied them. Some of the plants had clumped together and grass and reeds had taken root and grown and bound everything together until they became floating islands, some as long as 5 metres. There were eddies in the water and the islands were caught in these to waltz down the river until they were spun off to resume a more leisurely progress. Perhaps some of these plants were the ones that the horses had had to avoid on the Tipitapa river. Nearly every clump or island had a white egret on it, each bird standing tall on its private fishing raft. Buzzing past them, they took little notice of us though a few lifted off into the sky, folded their necks and glided to another spot, their legs pushed forward for landing.

There was a sudden, startling, splash in the water beside us and thoughts of crocodile crossed our minds, but we turned in time to glimpse two dorsal fins, a smooth creamy pink belly, and the flank of a fish, a big fish, a tarpon. This was our first sight of these animals that would become more common as we made our way down to Sábalos. Tarpon fishing is big sport but one thing was quite clear, not from this canoe, we would be tipped over at first bite.

Gazing at the river, tarpon spotting, watching for their curving bodies as they smoothly broke the surface of the water, I became aware of small, dark coloured, triangles floating around. We sneaked up on one and saw two small black, rather malevolent, eyes looking at us before the triangle sank down into the water. Although turtles were common and seemingly everywhere in the water, out of it we only saw a dozen or so, sitting on the banks or balanced on overhanging tree branches, on the entire trip.

Another fuel stop for the engine and we ate large slices of the watermelon that we had bought in the market in San

Carlos. Huge white clouds billowed into the sky ahead and promised rain. We would be at Sábalos within the next hour, if our maps and speed estimates had been right so we headed out to try to beat the weather. The clouds had got darker and the river was getting faster and the tarpon thicker. We sped around a bend in the river and saw, on our left our hotel, standing on stilts at the corner of the San Juan and the Sábalos rivers. We nosed into the steps of the hotel and tied up. The riverbank had been reinforced here as the town of Sábalos is a stop for all the ferry-boats and nothing can stop them powering their way around the bend into the Sábalos river and down to the town dock a hundred yards away. Their wash eats into the bank and would undermine the hotel if it were not for the reinforcing. Even so, mooring the canoe so that it was protected and would not crash into the wooden piles of the dock from the wash, took some thought.

We removed everything from the canoe and locked it away before relaxing with two Victoria beers on a veranda that stretched the whole length of the hotel and which overlooked the two rivers. Although tarpon are found along the whole length of the river, and in the lake, this is where most of them are found. We watched their continual rising and turning, bellies gleaming and fins cutting the surface. The Victoria was going down very well and we were pointing fish out to each other like children. The longest time we counted with no fish was 30 seconds! A brochure in the hotel tells us that the tarpon is more than 100 million years old and, like the bull shark can live in salt and fresh water. Females can live for 50 years whilst males lag behind at 35 years. They do not reach sexual maturity until they are 7-10 years old when they weigh about 40-60 pounds. The older and bigger they get the more eggs and sperm they produce. Most of their lives are spent in the river but from June to September they spawn in the sea when schools of them can be seen circling in the river mouth before moving offshore to lay their eggs, returning later to the river. They are an important food fish for the local population but are also a source of income from sport fishermen. The fighting of these huge fish, some weighing over 250 pounds, is legendary and makes them a fisherman's dream.

Just at the point where the Sábalos joins with the San Juan there were a group of canoes fishing. Men and boys stood at the front of the canoe and in one hand gathered up weighted circular nets that, without tipping the canoe, they threw out to unfold in the air and fall in circles into the water and, hopefully, on any unwary fish. They did seem to be catching a few so Joe decided to try his hand at fishing, "I hope I don't catch a tarpon!"

This proved not to be a problem as, in true angling tradition, he didn't catch anything! Cormorants were hanging out around the fishing but we could not decide which came first, were the cormorants following the fishermen or the fishermen the cormorants?

The hotel we stayed in had been built by a German gentleman and his daughter was running it, after spending two years in Germany. Was she going to stay?

"Maybe yes, maybe no."

At dinner we met a peace corps volunteer, a girl from Virginia who said that she was working with the women in the town, teaching them basic hygiene. But she said that it was very difficult as you taught them how to wash their hands one day and then you had to teach them all over again the next, and the next. My mention of birth control was met with a stony silence. Many of the Nicaraguan girls have their first child around fifteen and others duly follow, education is curtailed and any future that they might have is then limited. Deaths from childbirth are high and, if the mother dies, the family may disintegrate. Sábalos town swarms with bored children. We had already met a dozen or so similarly well-intentioned young women 'working with the women in the villages' and some do have very worthwhile projects that actually bring money, education and independence into the community but others seemed quite without any plan or practical support. We walked into the town later and saw half a dozen closed doors with logos on them ranging from 'health education' to 'save the forest' from various NGO's, many advertising the financial support given them from many different countries, but few signs of anything happening. We discovered that there were more NGO's per head of population in the Rio San Juan area than anywhere else in Nicaragua. We just hoped that the good and useful was being conducted behind closed doors, as there was no sign of it outside.

Sábalos is from where the huge logs came. They were taken from the forest to the river and loaded onto barges that travel to San Carlos every day. Also staying in the hotel was a man from MARENA the Nicaraguan Ministry of Environment and Natural Resources (Ministro de Medio Ambiente y Recursos Naturales). He told us that the wood being taken out of the forest was old wood that has been left to dry and that there was no more cutting of hardwoods in the area. Felling hardwood trees in a rainforest is not like cutting, say, a stand of oaks in Europe or North America. The rainforest hardwood species are scattered, and, for example, one mahogany tree to a hectare is considered a very good density. MARENA is desperately trying to control tree felling but they are so under-resourced and have so few people to keep track of what is happening in these, the largest wilderness areas in Central America that cover seventeen percent of Nicaragua. All wood now bought from lumber yards has been felled with permission, paid for and marked. There does seem to be some progress as woods that we were able to buy readily when we first arrived, are now almost impossible to obtain. But there are problems, one coming from Costa Rica, which has an uneasy relationship with Nicaragua over the San Juan. Another is the Indians and other people who live in and around the forests. Nearly one million people live in the Nicaraguan San Juan river basin and many of these fled into the forest to avoid the fighting during the last Sandanista/Contra war, whilst others were casually allotted bits of confiscated, or wild land. There is a programme to persuade these people away from the forest but, meanwhile, they have to earn a living. They are being offered high prices for illegally cut hardwoods some of which is taken to Costa Rica by any number of routes across the river.

    Next morning we took the canoe up the Sábalos river. The San Juan is fed by a huge water system. Most of the water comes from Lake Cociboloca which is fed by rivers and streams from the highlands of Nicaragua. Three large rivers, the Rios Bartolo, San Carlos and Sarapiqui flow into the river together with seventeen smaller rivers and many streams. The smaller rivers, like the Rio Sábalos, are perfect canoe rivers, the currents are not strong and it was easy to paddle and enjoy the scenery, the peace and listen to the birds, though the chattering conversations of parrots sometimes overwhelm the songbirds but they are beautiful and wondrous.

    A surprisingly large number of people live along the Sábalos in small shacks with banana plantations alongside but most of the people were in or on the river, washing clothes or themselves, children playing, boys fishing and men talking whilst lounging in and repairing canoes.

    The trees were immense and in places the branches touched across the river, a living tunnel. Howler monkeys called, their cries reverberating. Hard to imagine today the terrifying effect that their calls had on the early explorers. There were tempting side streams but we wanted to get on our way, down the San Juan, and not spend too much time exploring on this trip.

We paddled back to the town, manoeuvred around a lumber barge and avoided the cross-river ferry, a big canoe, about 30 feet in length with two people in it being rowed across the river by a girl of about eleven in a faded pink dress and long dark plaited hair. Another barge, this time packed with cattle, two cowboys and four dogs came towards us and, barely floating, a canoe paddled by four children in their white school shirts and blue skirts or trousers pulled into the town dock. We had seen them the evening before going back up the river against the current and assumed that they were doing their own school run. We moored next to them and Joe went on the hunt for fuel whilst I strolled through the town. There was only one street that went straight out of town to, we were told, an oil palm factory, though whether it was still working or not, we never found out. There were hairdressers, pulperias (tiny shops) some with rooms to let, restaurants with chicken and meat cooking on barbecues next to a few rough chairs and tables on an outside covered patio with maybe a plastic spoon as a concession to the gringos. A small market was stacked with fruits and vegetables; avocados just coming into season, enormous carrots and radishes, tomatoes and cabbages, sacks of rice and sugar; fish, meat and live chickens hanging by their legs. Three tall men were talking together each dressed in white shirts and dark trousers and Stetsons. Brothers, they could have been a mariachi band but were probably farmers. We saw them later sitting in the small palm leaf covered bar on the riverside by the dock as we pulled away down river back to our hotel.

Chapter 8   Reaching the Atlantic

The first set of rapids are just down the river from Sábalos and this was as far as Captain Ruy Dias reached on his first exploration in 1525. In 1529 Pedrarias put Martín Estete in charge of an expedition and he, too, was stopped by these rapids but he decided to abandon the river and he and his men cut their way through the forest to just a few miles from the Atlantic before he decided to return to Granada.

Pedrerias died in 1531 and his son in law, Rodrigo de Contreras, who was waiting for his appointment as governor to be approved, wanted to attempt the passage. However, he had defied crown orders prohibiting the ownership of slaves and was charged by Bartolome de la Casas who, even then, was defending the Indians against human rights abuses. Contreras went to Spain to seek vindication and get money together for an expedition but there were many delays and the impetus for the next exploration was the glint of gold.

In 1535 Queen Juana received a letter about the lake, the river and its access to the Atlantic, and gold, in quantities similar to the Yucatan and Moctezuma. This was before the outlet to the sea had been found, and the gold belonged more to imagination than reality   She ordered Contreras to explore the river as soon as possible but it took until 1539 to get everything organised and find competent men but eventually Captain Alonso Calero and Diego Machuca de Suazo, set forth from near Granada with one large boat carrying the animals, and seven other boats, included two lateen rigged lighters, one with fifteen rowing benches and the other with twelve, and four canoes; 100 soldiers, 40 horses, 50 pigs, some Indian bearers and a few priests. They launched with the horses in the boats but the lake was rough and the boats and the horses, which were very important for the expedition, were in danger, so they retreated to shore. The horses were

Rio San Juan

unloaded and they then went by land with Machuca. En route, they had to cross a river so, with the aid of a large cable slung across the river, everything was transported across, except the horses, which had to swim. After meeting up with the main party they all continued on together until Calero decided that he wanted to go to the Solentiname islands to find a guide, so he set off for there with twenty of his men. He and Machuca next met at the site of what would be San Carlos.

May 1st 1539 Machuca and Calero set off down the San Juan. This was the dry season when the river was at its lowest and the most difficult time to navigate it. The rocks were at their most dangerous and crocodiles and sharks plentiful. May 2nd they reached the El Toro rapids where they camped. Approaching El Toro, Calero went on to investigate when he saw four Indians fishing in the river. With help, he managed to sneak up on them and capture three of the Indians, two canoes and six fish that weighed a total of 300 pounds on which they all feasted that night.

Machuca, with 20 men, was sent to explore downstream and actually went through all the sets of rapids, El Toro, El Diablo and the third set that was to be named after him and is now known as the Machuca rapids. Learning that these were the last set of rapids, he returned up the river to talk with Calero and tell him that it would not be possible to take the larger boats. Calero decided that he wanted to see for himself so, with a priest and 40 men in four canoes set off down the San Juan and reached the entrance to the San Carlos river in two days, but then, paddling upstream, it took him five days to get back.

Machuca was now exploring up the Rio Sábalos and Calero, tired of waiting for him to get back, left a message to say that he would meet him at a village south of the Sarapiqui. One source tells that when Machuca came to the

El Toro rapids, he took his horses and some men to explore in the jungle but became hopelessly lost and ended up somewhere in the north of the country near the Rio Coco which is today the border with Honduras. There, they had to slaughter their horses for food but somehow managed to make their way back to Granada on foot. It is almost impossible to believe that this is what happened as it was a huge distance to travel at that time but it would explain why he was away so long and why Calero, in complete frustration, left.

Calero set off down river again but this time the El Diablo rapids lived up to their name and Calero's canoe capsized. He was rescued, which was just as well as he couldn't swim, but most of their firepower was lost. They continued on and safely navigated the Machuca rapids to arrive at the mouth of the Sarapiqui river. Finding enough food was a constant problem and here they raided an Indian village but found it abandoned and burning, the Indians long gone. They were more successful at another village further downstream but were still desperately short of food and far more interested in finding provisions than navigating the river. But all the while the river was taking them downstream until, suddenly, the Atlantic Ocean was before them. They were the first foreigners to travel the river and as they had arrived on 24th July, 1539, St. John's day, they named the bay San Juan. They had taken two months, man-hauled the boats over and around eight sets of rapids, and the prize was theirs. It had taken twenty years to find the route.

Chapter 9 Sábalos to El Castillo

Shortly after the Rio Sábalos enters the San Juan it narrows and flows faster down to the El Toro rapids.

We were getting ready to leave for El Castillo on a day that was just perfect, ideal weather and impressive scenery. We wondered if the early explorers had been as inspired as we were by the trees as they must have been even more magnificent when they were scouting the area, or were they too concerned about reaching the ocean, fame and fortune, and fearful of a river about which they knew little and were only too aware of the animals, real and perceived?

We were packing the canoe when the hotel owner came to talk to us and said that she was concerned about us taking the canoe through the El Toro rapids on our own without knowing the route as it was not easy to find and there were some very big rocks.

"We are going to El Castillo, why don't you just follow us?"

Joe reckoned that these rapids were not a real problem, and he was supported in his view by a couple of other people who had joined in the conversation. The water was high and although this meant that the river was flowing fast, the water was covering the rocks. The big problems came in the dry season. We had the route pointed out to us, and the places to keep clear of.

"Just look out for any rough patches and go around them." We were told.

We had watched boats of all sizes pass down the river ranging from a small dugout canoe paddled by a couple of children looking about eight years old, to the river ferry with its sixty passengers. The ferries were the largest boats to go on downstream past Sábalos, the log boats and cargo boats were not able to navigate any further and any goods going down the river had to be unloaded at Sábalos and transferred into lanchas for the trip over the rapids.

On our own we moved into the water and headed the canoe straight across the river towards the opposite bank as we had been taught. We then headed downstream and as far as possible we kept to the same route as the other boats. We kept a careful lookout for rocks and spotted a few large ones under the water but, by the time we had seen them, they were gone, the current had taken the canoe in its grip and rapidly pulled us past. There was little chance that we would be able to steer around any rocks but by watching for the rough water and avoiding it, one of the better bits of advice we got, we lurched through to the calmer water on the other side with no mishap.

Having passed El Toro rapids we decide to call into the Sábalos Lodge for a coffee. An 'eco' lodge with palm frond roofs, rooms open to the river and forest behind. The pony-tailed Nicaraguan owner caters to younger, more adventurous clients. He already had forest walks and horseback rides for his tourists but wanted to expand into kayak and canoe trips down the river and picked Joe's brains about our trip. He used to breed and export frogs, snakes and lizards to the US pet trade but the regulations are now so stringent and the licenses almost impossible to obtain that he had given it up in favour of tourism. (Though a later trip sees canoes lying idle and frogs in captivity.)

After coffee we strolled through the gardens and looked for the tame cat, of forest not domestic variety, but with no luck. We left Sábalos Lodge and crossed the river to the south bank to head over to another lodge, Monte Cristo. Developed by a Nicaraguan as a small fishing lodge it also has forest walks and horseback riding. We walked around trying to find someone and eventually the youngish

Rio San Juan

owner appeared with binoculars slung around his neck as he came from watching a sloth. He had spent time in the US as a navy mechanic and came back to Nicaragua after his father had died. He had used his inheritance to build the lodge and told us that it had been doing really well with clients mainly from the US. Doing so well that he did not have enough accommodation and built some more rooms. Then the trade tower disaster and his business completely collapsed with it. The gardens were lovely, planted with hundreds of fruit trees and was a bird watchers wonderland. We hoped that things would improve for him. (On a later trip Joe was happy to see that the lodge, if not full, was certainly busy.)

On the river again, the sun shone and light reflected off the leaves to make the forest gleam, gold, silver and red glinted amongst the foliage, and all was mirrored in the tea-coloured water. We heard monkeys and then, dogs. A bend in the river revealed a small coconut plantation and then a cattle ranch with fine, fat animals that Joe, the ex-rancher, said were a Brahmin/Charolais cross. The fields sloped upwards, with huge trees giving shade to the cattle until they too blended into the forest. Cowboys were moving the cattle, lassos coiled and at hand they eased themselves in their saddles.

The reflections of sky and forest on the river surface gave the illusion that you could just walk onto the water, but a bird took off, rippled the surface, and the deception was broken.

The river speeded up and a black and white bird with a red beak flew over the surface, scooping up water. This was a black skimmer, the lower part of the beak is much longer than the upper and when feeding and drinking it cuts into the surface of the water to scoop up water and any unsuspecting creature. They fly close to the water and make no disturbance as their wings never descend below the horizontal. This was the only one we saw on the entire trip.

Another bend and there were the stilted buildings of El Castillo.

Chapter 10   The Spanish, Pirates and The British on the River

The San Juan had been discovered and its exploration continued. Machuca eventually made it down the river to discover that he had not been abandoned by Calero as he had suspected. Calero had searched for him and left messages at the mouth of the river but eventually he had left with the fleet and gone to Nombre de Dios (in where is now Panama) where, instead of being welcomed, he was imprisoned, as the local President had predatory designs on the river himself. Calero managed to escape and found sanctuary in a church, if not freedom.   Machuca went to find him in Panama, discovered what had happened and decided to return up the river, and brought with him the first map of the river, its tributaries and rapids.

At this time, around the 1540s, Spain was using the land crossing to Nombre de Dios as the route for her South American riches but Queen Juana suggested that they change to the San Juan route.   Granada had a population of about 100 and trade was increasing.   Slaves, cotton, tobacco and sugarcane were all traded and Nicaragua, not having very much in the way of gold, turned to farming.   The rich volcanic soils produced abundant foodstuffs and indigo, tobacco, dye-woods, cochineal and flax joined the list of exports.

Indigo was an extremely valuable material but its production had almost completely stopped by the end of the 1800s. A bushel of seeds would plant up to five acres of land and the crop was ready to harvest in 2-3 months when the clover-like plant became coated in a greenish film.   It was cut with knives after which a second, better crop, would be ready later in the year.   The cut plants were bound in bundles and placed in layers in the top half of a vat.

Weighted boards were placed on the plants that were then covered with water and left to steep from between 6-20 hours. The water was then drawn off into the lower vat and beaten with paddles until it turned blue and had a tendency to curdle, after which it was allowed to settle and the excess water drawn off. The residue, similar to fine clay, was then placed in bags to drain and was then spread out to dry in the sun. The used plants, by law, had to be dried and burnt to destroy the indigo fly that bred in the debris by the millions.

Cochineal was an equally expensive product and Cortez, in 1523 was told to bring back as much as he could. A brilliant red, orange or pink dye it was derived from the cochineal insects that feed on cacti from where they are brushed off into bags and killed by heating. One pound of dye took seventy thousand insects.

Had the San Juan route succeeded it would have been strong competition for the Panama isthmus route and Robles, the same man who had imprisoned Calero, organised a force to colonise the mouth of the river and, once the ships had sailed, Calero was, at last, set free.

Meanwhile in Granada, with the help of Machuca, a unit was put together to evict these upstart colonists and, although the first attempt had to be abandoned due to one of the famous lake storms, on the second attempt they reached the mouth of the San Juan and Robles's fort where they laid siege and Robles surrendered. Machuca, who now had governor Contreras with him, met Calero coming up the river but Contreras distrusted Calero, had him arrested and sent to Granada. Later, new laws took away from Contreras many of his legitimate, authorised, money making rights which so incensed him that he went back to Spain to plead his case but he completely failed to get any largesse and when he later returned to Nicaragua in revenge he burned most of the boats

Rio San Juan

on the lake causing total chaos there and in most of western Nicaragua, before escaping to Panama.

The river was now in frequent use as there were ample supplies available and Indian bearers to carry them. In, 1544 it was suggested that the river should be made deeper to aid navigation and prevent casualties but nothing could be done to prevent ships being lost in the lake from the sudden storms and in the Atlantic at the mouth of the river. Besides trade the waterway was being used for all kinds of purposes; priests travelled it to save Indian souls and pirates to find treasure. Expeditions set forth along it to seek Montezuma's gold and to colonise Costa Rica. Of 380 men that went with one expedition, only 30 made it home, all sick and exhausted after lake storms, disease and disaster had taken their toll.

Trade was expanding and the river flourishing but so were the pirates. Spain had acquired a land route monopoly over the isthmus in Panama that was so profitable, and the retention of it considered so important, that the opening of any new routes, including all-water routes were forbidden; a stance that Spain held until the beginning of the 19th Century. A trail had been hacked out of the jungle and the mule trains that travelled it carried enormous quantities of gold and silver that were shipped to Spain. In the 1570s Nombre de Dios on the isthmus of Panama on the Spanish Main, that hot and humid, disease ridden Caribbean coast that stretches from Panama, along the whole Nicaraguan coast to Honduras, was the main treasure port. Twice a year Spanish galleons sailed into the harbour and dropped anchor. There they waited for shipments of gold and silver. The treasure ships were not protected and were easy, lucrative, prey for pirates and Francis Drake. Francis Drake had been in Nombre de Dios in 1571 when, in disguise, he had located the treasure house and befriended some Cimaroons, black escaped slaves who lived in the jungle and hated the Spanish.

Drake returned and made an ill-fated attempt to plunder the treasure house, attacking with drums and trumpets playing when they entered the town. But the Spanish were waiting and Drake received a serious thigh wound. A torrential rainstorm had them running for cover but their ammunition and bowstrings were soaked. They did reach the treasure house, Drake with blood pouring from his wound, but only to find it empty and the treasure fleet had sailed.

Drake was prepared to wait for the next shipment and give his leg a chance to heal and with his Cimaroon friends he explored the jungle and he too, saw the Pacific. He hoped that:

'God would spare him to sail in an English ship upon that glistening sea.'

He saw the treasure ships come from Peru and watched the gold and silver being packed onto mules and decided to ambush the train. But a drunken soldier gave the game away and alerted the enemy so it, too, came to nothing. After a disastrous Caribbean adventure, Francis Drake had designs on Granada to try to put something in his coffers before returning to England, but wrong winds and illness saved Granada that time.

Drake eventually fell in with a group of French who told him of three caravans of 190 mules each, all headed for Nombre de Dios. A joint French, British and Cimaroon attack was organised which successfully captured the mules, each of which carried 300 pounds weight of silver. Drake with his share of this treasure and loot from other raids along the coast sailed back to Elizabeth with £100,000 worth of gold and 15 tons of silver. The Spanish decided to abandon Nombre de Dios and transferred their treasure house to Portobello, further along the coast.

Drake returned in the Golden Hind declaring he could:

'...rob by command of the Queen of England'.

He circumnavigated the globe, he looted and plundered and captured the Cacafuego treasure ship which surrendered to him the equivalent of £12 million and which took some six days for the treasure to be transferred to the Golden Hind. With a total plunder of some £68 million he eventually returned to England and was knighted by Queen Elizabeth; he, his crew and his shareholders all ending up rich men. However, on a return trip to Portobello he fell ill and died in 1596.

Drake's place was soon taken by pirates, which included Henry Morgan, who were plundering the Caribbean coast of Central American and the Caribbean Islands.

By 1570 they were such a serious problem for Spanish ships in the Atlantic that trade shifted to the Pacific but there, too, the ships were not safe. Granada was, supposedly, free from pirate attacks as it was inland so goods were being sent there from all over Central America to go down river to the town of San Juan de Norte. But the pirates now had a base at Bluefields on the Atlantic making it easy for them to observe the shipping leaving the San Juan and a constant watch had to be kept before any ship would leave for Panama or Cartagena.

By 1590 Granada was thriving, larger than León the capital, it now had a shipyard building the riverboats. Gold, slaves and produce were traded and all this was as honey to the pirates and they started to pillage along the river. To try to establish some security, a fort, with a Spanish garrison was built just before the El Diablo rapids, on the site of El Castillo, and, in 1602 troops were placed at San Carlos to protect the ships, which included frigates of around 120 tons, that made the perilous and difficult passage down the San Juan from Granada to Spain, usually via Havana. In 1620 Spain wanted to make the rapids easier by removing rocks to help the trade goods traffic and also make it easier to transport troops along the river as they were skirmishing with the local Indians. At this time, 1621, it was possible for frigates to navigate the waterway as well as ships of 20 and 30 tons and in the rainy season, ships of over 100 tons. The rapids were always a problem, as was the bar at the mouth of the river. It took two months to travel the river, unloading and loading at each set of rapids. Freight sometimes had to be stored due to rain, passengers had to walk in extreme heat and sometimes pouring rain and always with mosquitoes. Many fell ill and some died. This year, too, was the first proposal, by a Guatemalan colonist, to build a canal across the strip of land between Lake Cocibolca and the Pacific.

England had recently taken Jamaica from Spain and English pirates were working out of the island with ease, and in Nicaragua, they were having a field day. The local Indians hated the Spanish and were more than happy to help the pirates who they allowed to travel freely, whereas the Spanish, they attacked. In the 1660s pirates controlled the mouth of the Rio San Juan and, possibly, as many as 500 buccaneers were living nearby.

A pirate is described as someone who robs and plunders on the sea, whilst buccaneers were pirates who operated in the 1600s in the Caribbean and the coasts of South and Central America but also included adventurers to whom any ship was prey. Then there were others, such as Henry Morgan who was technically a privateer as he was supported by his uncle, the English Governor of Jamaica, and held a 'letter of marque and reprisal' to attack and seize vessels of a hostile nation. For the English government, this was a cheap way of adding ships with experienced crews to fight for them and keep the seas for England, particularly as their pay was only whatever they could steal.

Pirates were one of the reasons why Thomas Gage in 1635 sought passage to Rome from Nicaragua rather than Honduras, which was the obvious choice. The Gulf of Honduras was so beset with Dutch pirates that trade goods from Guatemala, which would normally have left from Honduras, were being sent to Granada. Gage had already discovered that the lake passage would be easy but that it could take two months to get down the San Juan, loading and unloading cargo, that the gnats (lake flies, mosquitoes) were intolerable and passengers known to have died of heat before they reached the sea. Gage obtained a passage but, a couple of days before leaving, news arrived that the frigates should not leave that year as pirate ships were in wait for them in the San Juan. Gage gave up and left Granada to go to Panama to seek passage from there, getting his encounter with the crocodile on the way.

It was only a matter of time before pirates reached Granada but nature intervened. There had been earlier earthquakes, notably one in 1648 that left a Spanish brigatine stranded but the 1663 earthquake changed the river quite radically for the worse and made navigation much more difficult. Big ships could no longer navigate the river and one frigate (not to be confused with a frigate of today, it was a small ship of between 80-120tons) was trapped in the lake, never to leave again.

Earthquakes did not deter the pirates who homed in on Granada however Edward Hume who:

'...valued as but the price of a bottle of wine all the loot of Granada in comparison with the privilege of having seen the city and the lake with its isletas and the island of Omotepe.'

And:

'...vowed to do everything in his power to persuade either the English or the Portuguese to give him men, ships and arms to take and hold the ports of the lake from which a connection with the South Seas could so easily be made'.

But these opinions did not stop him and 140 men sacking and burning Granada on June 29th 1665 at two o'clock in the afternoon.

John Davis and Henry Morgan made a daring attack on Granada after a difficult and dangerous journey, cutting their way through the forest and reaching Granada with 40 men at two o'clock one morning. They had hidden out during the day but paddled over to the town that night and totally surprised the quite unprepared inhabitants. They sacked it of its gold and riches, burnt any boats they found, and left. The prize was great.

The story of Henry Morgan is fantastic, far too long for here but the following exploits give an idea. He was born around 1635 a Welsh gentleman's son and went with an expedition sent by Oliver Cromwell and under General Venables to harry the Spanish. The expedition was something of a disaster even though it did capture Jamaica, but that was not quite what England had in mind. It was thinking more along the lines of Vera Cruz, Havana or Cartagena and Venables ended up in the Tower of London on his return to England.

Jamaica was terrible, the English dying in droves of dysentery, yellow fever and malaria and by the hands of the Spanish and the maroons – runaway slaves in the forests of the island. In 1662 Morgan appears as captain of a ship under Commodore Myngs and was courageous and successful during the next years although something of an alcoholic. He was so good at his job that he was appointed "Admiral" by the group of pirates known as the buccaneers, The Brethren of the Coast.

Morgan wanted to attack Cartagena but en-route met Vice-Admiral Alonsa del Campo y Espinosa with three well-armed men of war. Morgan ordered a small, unmanned ship to sail towards them, an event that was ignored by the galleons until it exploded, burning one ship, causing the second to flee whilst the third was captured. Morgan was inside the lagoon of Maracaibo but Espinosa had managed to get to a fort on an island that commanded the entrance to the lagoon. Morgan was trapped, but he tried a ruse. Whilst many of his men were raising the treasure from Espinosa's ship in the lagoon, Morgan pretended to prepare to attack the fort from the land. The pirates were rowed across the bay to the land sitting upright in the boat and back, lying down. The same pirates rowed across and back, again and again. The ruse worked, Espinosa ordered the guns to be turned towards the land. Morgan waited for the ebb tide, weighed anchors and sailed away, with the treasure.

His escapade at Portobello in Panama is legendary but he did get into trouble there trying to capture the silver and gold sent from the mines in Peru as, after a short fight, he found that it had all been moved. Worse, Spain was furious with him as they were no longer at war with England and demanded that Morgan be imprisoned. Reluctantly,

Morgan was sent back as a prisoner to England but he never saw the inside of the Tower. Holland was now the enemy and they were attacking Jamaica, which was having trouble keeping the Dutch at bay. Charles II asked Morgan for his advice and he made such a good impression on the king that he was knighted and sent back to Jamaica as Governor, Vice-Admiral, Commandant of the Port Royal Regiment, Judge of the Admiralty Court and Justice of the Peace. He was 34 years old.

Morgan and his men made fortunes. They were very wealthy men and Morgan, who had married his cousin and remained happily with her all his life, had sugar plantations in Jamaica and lived there until his death in 1687, rather ingloriously of 'dropsy and years of dissolute living'.

When Morgan took off with £500,000 down the Rio San Juan, enough was enough. A defence tower was built at El Castillo in 1666 and rocks were thrown into the rapids in an attempt to make them impassable. To protect Granada and control the lake traffic, a fort was built near San Carlos However, in 1670 this fort was taken and burnt by pirates who then went on to Granada to plunder there yet again. Something had to be done and the El Castillo site above the rapids at El Diablo was considered the strategically most important point on the river with views both up and down. Construction of the fort El Castillo de la Inmaculada Concepción began. The largest defensive structure in Central America it was 90 feet wide, 195 feet long with walls four feet thick, a drawbridge and a moat. It boasted fourteen cannon, stone-throwers, and more than 100 men. An additional nine defensive positions were built along the river that successfully deterred 'invasions' for more than a century.

Granada now was weakened and hearing that buccaneers were in control of the river, the people moved out and the town was left with a population of about twelve Spanish and some natives. Even so, buccaneers attacked again, this time from the Pacific in the person of William Dampier. Granada was prepared but the small population was easily overrun, and in any case there was little to loot as any valuables left had been safely hidden in ships in the middle of the lake. After burning eighteen big houses, and the Iglesia San Francisco, the buccaneers retreated to the lake with only three men lost.

It is thought that in 1720 there were some 2,000 pirates active in the Caribbean and trade was almost at a standstill. A number of measures were put into effect to drive them off that included pardons, more naval ships and rewards for capture on the one side, and executions on the other. It would take until the mid 1700s for Granada's trade to recover.

The British were then the problem. The Indian's hatred of the Spanish worked to the advantage of the British forces, as it had for the pirates. The Crown recognised the Misquito kingdom on the Atlantic coast as a separate nation, acknowledged their king and armed them to fight against the Spanish. The Misquitos caused all kinds of problems in the region, they harried the river boats, attacked any ships sent to engage them, including four ships with 125 men and equipped with stone-throwers who were so intimidated by them that they refused to fight. However, the Misquitos were later overpowered by the Spanish in a short confrontation near the mouth of the Rio Colorado. More garrisons were set up along the San Juan and by 1727 there were a total of twelve but due to cost-cutting El Castillo was the only defense left in 1745.

In the 1750s Granada had 600 houses, 400 with tile roofs and a wide street from the lake to the town with four north/south streets and others intersecting. This is the same pattern that the old centre of the town has today and might well be recognised by someone from that time.

Granada was again beginning to thrive, partly due to a contraband trade between the British and the Indians that included chocolate. Cacao was an important crop. After planting it took seven years before the first cocoa pods appeared but the trees then bore two crops a year for 30-50 years. Nicaraguan cocoa was extremely good and a high-yield crop but by the mid 1850s production had greatly decreased. (More recently cocoa blight stopped production altogether but some trees have been replanted and today chocolate is again being farmed.)

Britain and Spain were at war again and this time it spilled into Nicaragua with the British and the Indians ascending the river and attacking El Castillo. The defeated commander of the fort had died and the garrison was about to surrender but his teenage daughter, Rafaela Herrara, who had been taught to shoot by her father, took over the command of the fort. She rallied the men and prepared for battle. She fired the first cannon shot herself and, so the story goes, on her third shot killed a British captain. The battle continued for 5 days until one dark night under heavy attack and unable to see the enemy boats she ordered sheets to be soaked in alcohol, hung in the trees and set alight thereby illuminating the river for her cannon. The fires had the additional effect of burning branches that fell into the water and were carried by the fast flowing river down to the British wooden boats, which were forced to retreat. Rafaela was awarded a lifetime pension by the Spanish Crown and is still a heroine of the Nicaraguan people.

Rio San Juan

The British retreated but remained at the mouth of the Rio San Juan and, aided by their Misquito allies, prevented ships entering the river, particularly those carrying reinforcements from Spain.

By the 1770s Spain controlled the whole of the Americas and Britain was keen to break this Spanish monopoly and obtain access to a route across the isthmus for its own trade with the far east and take a share of the lucrative contraband trade from the Pacific ports of Central and South America. By taking the San Juan and Lake Cocibolca, Britain would cut the Spanish holdings in half and secure the trans-isthmus route for itself. Britain still had its Misquito allies on the Nicaragua coast and they would help with any attack to take the San Juan.

Spain knew what was happening and sent an envoy, an American colonist, to make peace with the Misquitoes. Everything went well and a settlement was founded near the mouth of the San Juan. But something went dreadfully wrong between Indian and Spanish relations with the result that nearly all the settlers were killed.

El Castillo had been repaired and overhauled and now had 40 cannon and about 300 men. A British attack plan was devised and a small, armed fleet was to ascend the San Juan in flat-bottomed boats and capture El Castillo; continue to the lake and establish a port from where to cross the land isthmus. This obvious plan was approved.

On February 7th 1780 two troop transport ships left Jamaica for Gracias a Dios on the northernmost tip of Nicaragua under the protection of the Hinchbrooke. One of the ships was a frigate carrying 500 men and commanded by a young, 22 year old Horatio Nelson. They reached Gracia a Dios where, and this was to prove disastrous for them, they waited for reinforcements to arrive. The Mosquito Coast is one of the unhealthiest places on earth, more swamp than land and the men contracted malaria, yellow fever, dysentery and other illnesses. Once the reinforcements arrived they all headed down the coast to San Juan del Norte. It was the 1st April before they headed up-river. There was no sign of any of the flat-bottomed boats that they had been promised, so canoes and the longboats from the Hinchbrooke were used to ascend the river. It was the dry season and some of the boats were totally unsuitable and required constant pushing and pulling to get them over the sandbars that were always a navigational problem near the mouth of the San Juan. Passage was slow and frustrating. The forest stretched down to the river banks and loomed overhead; there were swarms of mosquitoes and other insects but the men were more frightened of the crocodiles and sharks in the river and the snakes, jaguars and other cats in the jungle and the then unknown origin of the terrifying calls of the howler monkeys. There are many islands along this part of the river, some quite large, and as they neared El Castillo they were attacked by the Spanish from a battery on one of these islands but this proved to be nothing more than an inconvenience to the British and a platoon, including Nelson, stormed and over-ran it. They then continued to El Castillo and camped just east of the fort.

One group set out for San Carlos to take the fort there, whilst the rest prepared to attack El Castillo. Nelson wanted to go ahead and storm the El Castillo fort and get it over with, but his Colonel in charge decided on a siege. Armaments were positioned on an overlooking hill, since then known as Nelson's Hill, and three weeks later the fort had surrendered with its 220 men. Nelson, however, had by then retreated down river almost dead from dysentery and disease, illnesses that took him more than a year to recover from. Had he stayed in Nicaragua he may well have died, and history might have been very different. Folklore has it that Nelson lost either his eye or arm, depending on the source, at the siege of Castillo. Neither is true, he left as intact as he arrived, but later damaged his eye off Corsica and lost his arm at Tenerife.

The British having succeeded in their aim now had to keep the forts. During the next weeks El Castillo had to be defended and the fort at San Carlos reinforced, but there were no fit soldiers, many were dead, all the survivors ill. From the first moment that they arrived in Nicaragua they were beset with illness. Malaria and yellow fever from mosquito bites, dysentery from unclean water. They endured bites from snakes and even a jaguar attack and eventually there were not even enough able bodied men to bury the dead, many of whom were just left for the crocodiles, caimans, sharks, vultures, and other scavengers.

By the end of the year El Castillo was back in Nicaraguan/Spanish hands. The British defeated by starvation, disease, climate and poisonous reptiles.

After the ease with which the British took El Castillo, it was downgraded as a fort but was still used to defend the river from the Misquito Indians who were still raiding up and down its length. San Carlos took over the main job of protecting the Rio San Juan.

Chapter 11   El Castillo and El Diablo

El Castillo is a small town with brightly coloured, tin roofed, buildings perched on wooden stilts over and along the river with canoes and lanchas moored underneath.   It is squeezed onto a strip of land with the river on one side and a hill on the other leaving just enough room for one road, and is today an attractive town.   But Thomas Belt on his trip in 1873 declared that:

> 'The sparkling, dancing rapids on one side contrast with the still, dark forest, on the other…. This view is the only pleasant recollection I have carried away of the place. The single street is narrow, dusty and rugged, and when the shades of evening begin to creep up, swarms of mosquitoes issue forth to buzz and bite.'

The earth mound with the surprisingly large remains of fort El Castillo still dominates the town.   With no roads and no cars, only horse trails, trade and passage is focussed on the river and the dock at El Castillo, which is right in the middle of the town, is where all the action is.

We pulled our canoe into the dock, dodged the children diving into the water, and went for a stroll around the town, which has a languor about it.   We walked up the grass-covered hillock on which the remains of the 350 year-old fort still stand and admired the spectacular views of the winding river, both upstream and downstream.   We gazed at the El Diablo rapids immediately below us and listened to them. There is nowhere in the town where you cannot hear the sound of the rapids.   We stared at them and watched boats zigzagging through them.   It looked hazardous and we wondered about just carrying everything, including the canoe the 50 metres or so around them and giving them a miss.

Rio San Juan

There would be no shortage of helping hands for a few cordobas each. But we decided that it would be copping-out to not go down them. At least it was no longer the crocodile and shark infested spot of the past, was it?

A chicken and chips lunch at a restaurant overhanging the river from where we could watch the boats crossing the rapids. I was getting decidedly uneasy, Joe was more casual.

"They do it all the time, it can't be that much of a problem. The water is high and you don't have to be quite as careful as in the dry season when the water is low."

"So what are all those rocks sticking up out of the water then?" I testily remarked stabbing a fork in the air towards them.

"The fact that you can see them means you can keep clear of them."

No point in hanging around, we piled into the canoe and pushed off. We crossed to the opposite bank of the river, as had the boats we'd been watching, and moved into the rapids, the water swifter than we had expected, moving very fast and we had little chance of controlling the canoe. Much too fast to avoid any rocks and, suddenly, we were stuck fast, the canoe settled right on top of a rock. We tried to dislodge it but, of course, inevitably, over it went and everything with it. We surfaced, then thrashed about trying to find some balance and stability in the water yet not let go of the canoe as it was the only thing we had to hang onto as the rocks were covered with algae and very slippery. We slid down the river and watched everything drift away, but we lunged after gas cans, paddles and anything else we could grab. I tried to turn the canoe right-side up and to my surprise, it flipped over easily and we threw anything we could find into it, slipping underwater every now and then as our feet slid off the rocks. At least the water was warm!

We were rescued by another boat with three men that had been going through the rapids at about the same time as us and which we had, unsuccessfully, tried to follow. They had collected most of our stuff and guided us into calmer water where everything was transferred to the canoe and, holding it steady, we climbed back in. We baled it out and the only obvious casualties were a hat that Joe had bought in Namibia, that was not going to be easy to replace, an umbrella and two beautiful mangoes that we had been given at Monte Cristo lodge. Joe tried the engine and, amazingly, it started on his first pull. Our rescuers made sure that we were all right and then sent us on our way, us having been the cause of much entertainment to the whole population of El Castillo. But we also espied our mangoes in the bottom of their boat, a cheap price for their help!

El Diablo had lived up to its name and although it would not count on any
white-water canoeing scale, it was quite enough to prove a nuisance to us, as it had to those who had travelled it earlier.

Chapter 12 Bartola to Trinidad

Everything was soaked, including ourselves, but it was not far to Bartola lodge on the north bank of the river where we arrived like drowned rats. We had not booked and hoped that they would have space and, as the most up-market and expensive lodge on the river, except for a fishing lodge at San Juan del Norte, hoped that they would have us. Happily, there was no-one else staying and we were able to assess the damage. The plastic box proved totally non-waterproof with everything in it, floating. We soon had the lodges' clotheslines festooned with wet clothes, mosquito net, passports, shoes, ropes and books, Bill Bryson's 'A Short History of Nearly Everything' would never be the same again whilst my Kipling's 'Plain Tales from the Hills' came off somewhat better (thinner). My bag, which was inside a thick black plastic bag, was just damp rather than saturated. My notes survived as did the birdbook, but the binoculars never recovered. The loss of Joe's hat was worrying as hats were essential as there is no escape from the sun. We were already burnt even though we had been liberal with the x20 sunscreen. Thankfully Joe unearthed a spare baseball cap that he hung up to dry along with everything else.

Bartola lodge is partly used as a research station but the laboratory building and boat looked very sad and neglected but in a wet hot climate mould appears in a matter of days on any uncared for equipment. A group of scientists were expected shortly so maybe they would breathe life back into the base. It was a perfect situation for field biologists as it had both river and forest. The lodge itself backs onto forest so, while waiting for things to dry, we set off with a map to go for a walk. The map proved quite useless as we kept ending up at the same cross paths and after a while we were even starting to recognise individual tree roots that we had had to climb over in our meanderings. After about an hour we decided to head back to the lodge when we heard a tell-tale rustling in the tree tops and came upon a family of spider monkeys. Amazing animals, we watched their acrobatics; they walked along a branch, hooked their tails around another and swung upside down, their enormously long arms reaching out for leaves, fruit or flowers or, just something to steady themselves on to stare at us, or push off to swing. We watched them for as long as they hung around, seemingly quite unconcerned by our presence.

The lodge has its own spider monkey, a female, Daniela, who loves men and hates women. She had been found in the forest next to her dead mother and now she had a home in the lodge. She wore a collar to which a long chain was attached with the other end fastened in a tree so she had a lot of space on the ground and in the tree in which to move around. Sometimes, when there were no guests, she was left loose, but a very close eye was kept on her as those long searching arms and hands can reach into all kinds of spaces and get into all kinds of mischief. A primate research camp in Kenya where I had stayed many years earlier had found that one of the most common causes of death among monkeys, though more commonly amongst young ones rather than adults, was falling out of trees and maybe this was what had happened to Daniela's mother.

Back at the lodge our clothes had dried nicely and we turned some pages in the books, which were swelling as they dried. We headed for showers, then went on the search for beers. There were only a couple of people working at the lodge and, with many apologies, broke the news to us that there was no beer and, not much food either! The owner was shopping in San Carlos and would be back tomorrow. However, we dined in a palm covered patio overlooking the river on typical Nicaraguan fare of beans and rice mixed with onions and peppers, an omelette, fried cheese, platano and an

Rio San Juan

avocado salad. A bottle of Flor de Caña rum had weathered the rapids, and there was cola at the lodge, so, all in all, not bad at all. We finished the evening looking out over the river watching the fireflies, tracking them by their flashes through the dark reeds.

Next morning the sun was shining and we decided to stay another day to try to get everything really dry and see something more of the forest. The lodge is situated on a corner where the Rio Bartola flows into the San Juan and we took the canoe to explore a little way up the Bartola. This river is one of the boundaries of the huge Indo-Maiz protected area, Central America's second largest nature reserve and the biggest primary rain forest; 3,618 square kilometres it covers a large part of SE Nicaragua. The western border is the Rio Bartola, the Rio San Juan the south, the Caribbean the east and Punta Gorda the north. Possibly, one of the largest areas of uncut rainforest north of the Amazon basin with trees over 50 metres in height the reserve has other habitats that include huge wetlands with rivers, dry tropical coastal forest, and pristine cloud forest. There is a range of volcanoes and some enormous annual rainfalls, 3,000 millimetres on the west and 5,000 millimetres at the Caribbean. Very little scientific work has been conducted but what is known is remarkable, 600 bird species, 300 reptiles and amphibia, 200 mammals and the insects, completely unknown. It is a treasure trove for any insect taxonomist.

We left the lodge and crossed over to the opposite bank of the Bartola where MARENA has an office and where every boat coming or going along the Bartola and the San Juan has to check in. All logging is controlled, most of it completely forbidden, and these check points along the river are one of the front line positions in curbing illegal logging. Leaves and pink flowers floated on the surface with a mirror image in the water. We were close to the bank and saw a line of leaf-cutter ants marching along, each with an umbrella of pink petal, to take to their nest. The nests are huge and can stretch for as much as 50 metres. In any one nest there are 5 million workers ranging in size from 2 millimetres to big soldiers at 20 millimetres. The middle-sized ants, about 10 millimetres, are the ones you see doing all the leaf and flower cutting and carrying, taking their loads home. There, the small ants take over and clean and scrape the surface of the leaf or flower pieces to remove any wrong fungi. They then cut them into even smaller bits, chew them, mix them with saliva and manure them with faeces to form a paste like mass that is then placed in the fungus garden. A few fungal strands are added, which quickly grow to form a mat, and then the strands form swollen tips that are collected by the ants for food. Should the queen ant have to move and start a new colony she will make sure that some of her precious fungus goes too.

A kingfisher streaked by and there was a chattering from the forest. We were paddling and the silence was golden, just jungle noises and small splashes, a scene unchanged for hundreds of years. This is one of the world's unknown backwaters, there are no other people, just the slightly menacing forest and strange screams somewhere in the depths. We pulled into a small pier sticking out into the river intending to tie up to it but the piles were rotting and most of the planking missing so, instead, we nosed into the bank, scrambled up and tied onto a tree. This was the start of the only trail into the Indo-Maiz reserve and, although Nicaragua would like the money, they are trying to make sure that opening up the reserve to tourists is done very carefully, without the damage that can be seen in other places. After only a few steps into the forest, the strange calls were revealed as coming from spider monkeys, a small group hanging around, literally, in the trees at the top of the bank. These were different to the ones we had seen earlier, bigger and darker. A male looked at us, hanging upside down he was holding on with just his tail and chewing on some fruit he was holding in his hands. After a cursory examination, he threw the fruit away, swung upside up, defecated, and was off with the others into the forest. Spider monkeys are not as common as the howlers and we felt very fortunate to have seen two species.

The wet lowland rain forest was dramatic and, although the dock was a bit of a let down, the trail itself with bridges over deep ravines and plenty of seats that encouraged us to stop and stare and listen, were excellent. Huge trees towered skyward, branches crowded with epiphytes. In the high cloud forests elsewhere, epiphytes cover every available space on their supporting tree, from topmost branch to trunk and as they use the water from the vapour in these cloudy realms everything is sopping wet. The weight of the water can be so much that the tree can no longer support its guests and it topples to the ground, crashing through vegetation as it falls and crumbles. Here, in this low-lying rain forest there are fewer epiphytes than in the high forests but the many large bromeliads are home to many animals, the pools of water at the base of their leaves perfect for frogs and tadpoles, salamanders, small snakes and other animals that have adapted to this exotic habitat.

The forest stretched away and huge butterflies danced through the air, blue morphos and owl butterflies with eyed wings. Dragonflies hurtled around and we saw occasional birds. This place is always going to be difficult to get to and that may be its saving. Reluctantly, but promising ourselves that we would return, we walked back along the trail, startling a green and black poison-arrow frog on the way. Their poison used to tip Indian arrows but now, like all amphibia, they are extremely protected but sadly something is killing frogs, seemingly everywhere. They are extremely good parents and have been observed taking the tiny tadpole to water, often the pool in a bromeliad plant. In one species the tadpole, when the adult female frog comes near, stiffens its tail and vibrates it which causes the adult to produce an unfertilised egg for food for the tadpole. This behaviour may or may not be true of all poison arrow frogs, but it is absolutely unique, unknown in any other vertebrate.

We paddled back to the lodge and discovered that the boat had arrived with supplies. We were greeted by the owner who had a big broad grin on her face as she told us all about our exploit at the rapids! It turned out that everybody on the river knew about our mishap but they were all just amused by it and nobody was critical. A rearrangement of drying clothes, more pages of Bill Bryson turned, they were sticking a bit but he would like this I thought. Kipling was faring better. Supper was wonderful; gazpacho, huge river shrimps, fresh salad, fruits and beer! We watched more fireflies, listened to the splashes in the water and then made our way to bed, dodging large warty toads on the way. We arranged the mosquito net and collapsed into instant sleep.

The river was blanketed in fog the next morning but by 7.30 a.m., it was dissipating and slowly lifting over the trees, unwrapping them from trunk to topmost leaf. The huge palm tree fronds were dragged down by the water drops and howler monkeys started their morning roll call. The river was very wide here and very calm, the current slow, the only movement the ghostly passage of the vegetable islands.

Our clothes were now as dry as they were going to get and this time we tied everything onto the canoe and, before putting things into the non-waterproof plastic box, put them into plastic bin liners.

The weather was glowering, a dark grey sky had been revealed when the fog lifted and clouds were building downriver, there was even a ruffle of wind. At least the sun was less of a problem. The evening before, in conversation with the Nicaraguan woman owner and one of the men who worked for her, it had been decided that we had to follow a boat through the Machuca rapids. Although not so steep as El Diablo, they are nearly three kilometres long and the route through them, tortuous with water flowing rapidly.

This time we took the advice and followed a wooden canoe that set off in front of us. We checked in at the MARENA office at the edge of the forest before attacking the rapids. With strict instructions to keep exactly behind the canoe, we set off. It was some distance to the rapids but we could see water breaking over rocks before we reached them. The main stream of the river seemed to be the channel we were taking and our canoe was having no difficulty in getting through. If this was all there was to it then all we needed to have been told was to follow this main flow of water.

The canoe in front pulled into a bank and asked if we were all right and happy to go further. Of course we were, we were through the rapids, no problem and now, off we go.

"It might be a bit rough, stay very close to us."

We then realised that what we thought were the rapids were just the straggling start and that the main stretch was still to come. Moving back into the river and around a bend it all became very clear. The water was churning, and the wind was getting stronger. The main channel was completely invisible and we stuck right behind the bigger canoe, moving over now and again according to their directions to keep exactly in their wake. We moved downstream, zigzagging our way across the river, Joe steering with difficulty to prevent the canoe being pushed and pulled off our route by the current and rough water, yet not tip us over.   About two kilometres later we were through and into calmer water.

Another pause on the bank and, with many thanks to our pilots, we cheerily waved goodbye, they to go back to Bartola and us, downstream with more respect for the river as we realised that we would probably not have managed the rapids on our own, and that there was nobody around to rescue us if we did capsize.

The river was now very wide and the two banks distinctly different. The north bank belongs to Nicaragua and is all part of the huge Indo-Maiz reserve whilst the south bank belongs to Costa Rica and is predominately cattle ranches, at least one large hacienda with verandas, gardens, stables and a Land Rover, our beloved vehicle of past adventures. We passed various houses and small coconut and banana plantations, and more ranches   Further east the banana plantations are huge and remaining forest is being sacrificed to expand them.   Banana production uses enormous amounts of insecticides that leak into the extensive water system and there are real worries that they are leaking into the San Juan and might be harming the eco-system.

We pulled into the Costa Rica bank for yet another energy bar (these were getting really boring) another bottle of water and we scared a bright green Jesus Christ lizard which, like a small dinosaur with head and tail held high, scampered across the water.   Nervous about the weather we filled up our petrol tank and pushed away from the bank.

The north side is forest all the way and after hours passing it you get some idea of the extent of this reserve. The vegetation completely hid the banks of the river and the variety, completely bewildering. Thomas Belt declaring:

'infinite variety....they crowd together in unsocial rivalry'.

There were large rather forbidding palms, their huge dark leaves reaching almost to the ground they exuded nothing of the frivolity of some of their relations. There were stands of cane, similar to the species that is used extensively in the ceilings of the colonial houses, our house took 40 fletas. (25 pieces of cane in a roll, 42 rolls in a fleta). When you multiply that by all the houses being renovated in Granada alone, huge quantities of cane are being used.

The tea coloured river was still, except where the vegetable islands were congregated in the main current and floated along, surrounded by foam from the rapids. The birds were hiding, a single heron here and there but nothing like the numbers at the start of the river, an occasional cormorant, a few anhingas hanging out, and a flash of a kingfisher or jacana.

The butterflies were still crossing the river and a huge bee, black and beige, became attracted to the canoe. It would fly to the absolute front of the canoe and buzz around, not quite alighting, for a minute or so and then fly off to return a few minutes later. It stayed with us nearly the whole of that day, and the next, and whether it was just one bee or a succession of different ones, I have no idea, but we missed it when it finally abandoned us.

We had one more police/MARENA check point on this stretch of the river at the Refugio Vida Silvestre, part of the Indo-Maiz reserve. A quick look at passports and we were waved on our way. Back on the river, we stopped soon after for refuelling, and drifted very slowly downstream with a following wind helping to push us along. The weather was worsening, ahead the clouds were climbing and looked threatening, and the first drops of rain had fallen. Out came the waterproofs, not so much to keep us dry but to keep warm as, even in this temperature, it can get cold when wet and windy.

The wind was rapidly strengthening and Joe was having difficulty keeping the canoe on a straight line. The river, which only moments before had been flat calm, was now covered with waves, and these, together with the wind, were buffeting the canoe and trying to push it off its course. The waves were irregular and although the canoe bobbed into them all right, they were breaking over the boat, and us; Joe was steering with one hand and bailing with the other. It was raining heavily now and visibility getting worse. Great huge drops of rain plopped into the water, a ripple formed around each drop with a tiny water volcano in the middle, a bit like watching a slow motion film. Then the rain was battering down, within ten minutes we had gone from a reasonable day to a storm. Thunder was rumbling and lightening forked out of the clouds. A conversation about being on a river in an aluminium boat in an electric storm was enough for me to persuade Joe that we just had to retreat to a bank and sit it out. We pushed under some trees and scrambled out of the canoe, to sit and wait. The fact that, on top of being soaking wet, we were covered with mud after climbing up the bank, just didn't seem to matter, it was just a relief to get away from the waves. We had pulled up to a cattle ranch and were being observed by some very bewildered calves, also trying to shelter from the rain.

Rio San Juan

Having dried everything out after capsizing, it would be interesting to see just how wet everything was after today.

The storm moved away almost as quickly as it had arrived but it was still raining and we were cold and uncomfortable. La Trinidad on the Sarapiqui river was our next stop and we knew that it was not so very far so we headed back into the river to try to get there as soon as possible. This was one of the widest sections of the river and we were puttering along at full speed when there was a sudden grating noise, and an equally sudden, stop. The rain had made us careless and we were on a sandbar. Paddles out, we pushed ourselves off and, rather more cautiously, navigated our way between the sandbanks. We now knew why so many of the dugout canoes we had seen had poles as well as paddles.

With relief we arrived at the mouth of the Sarapiqui, a wide, fast-flowing, muddy river that originates in Costa Rica and which was pouring water into the San Juan. The confluence of this surge of water was making things very difficult for the canoe and, to make things even more complicated, there was a huge sunken log between us, and the pier at the check station on the Nicaraguan bank. We had to check in there before heading across the river to the Costa Rican side and La Trinidad where we were going to spend the night. A policeman pointed out to us the best route to get around the log, which was causing strong eddies in the water. We turned around and moved slowly back upstream, the engine at full throttle, to get far enough away from the log to turn the canoe so that we would be between the log and the bank when we came back down. When we thought that we far enough upstream, Joe turned the canoe for the second attempt and we skidded down, kept close to the bank, missed the log by a graze, and just managed to catch the pier before being carried off down river. The pier was at the bottom of a greasy mud bank leading to the MARENA and police station, almost impossible to climb with all the rain, but we were already covered in so much mud that a bit more didn't make much difference. You would have thought that they would have put some steps in for their own sakes. My British passport caused some confusion and they stamped me out of Nicaragua, then they decided that they didn't have to do that so cancelled it. Joe's US passport had more or less dried out and together with his residency he had no problem.

We slid back down the bank and into the canoe and headed upstream again, partly to avoid the log but also to get high enough up river before crossing over to the opposite bank, to get to the Costa Rica police station and border post just inside the Sarapiqui, and not be swept away at speed, past the post, past the river mouth and on down the San Juan. The engine was furiously working and pushing us through the water, waves were breaking over us, and the propeller was sometimes right out of the water, but more or less keeping us on track. We made it to the police station and there was the same scramble up another mud bank. I had been here about 20 years earlier and it all looked just the same. I had stayed at a forest lodge down the Sarapiqui and we had taken cigarettes and some other goodies over to the Nicaraguan border guards before a safari down the river and they had turned out to be bored teenagers with guns. They were grateful for the cigarettes and the food we had brought as they clearly had very little and then asked if there was any chance that the Costa Ricans would like to play basketball with them. The request was turned down then but later basketball, soccer and baseball games were regular engagements.

On the opposite bank to the police station was La Trinidad. This was the position of one of the garrisons stationed along the San Juan. In the 1800s travellers commented on the lack of farming and remarked on the closeness of 'tigers' but settlers began to move in and in the mid 1800s, a German with forethought, cleared the land here, planted fruits and vegetables and opened an hotel and restaurant. We battled across the river and moored on a proper dock, with a proper path leading to the small hotel that caters to the tourists that manage to get that far. Most of these come via Costa Rica and use the Sarapiqui, San Juan and Colorado rivers route to get to the Atlantic turtle beaches and wetland area of Tortuguera.

We checked in, took everything out of the boat and carried it all up to our rooms with some help from a couple of sulky boys. We tied the boat up but were advised that we should lengthen the rope. All we wanted was a shower and mine, if not hot, was at least warm. The water heater was of the suicide type, an electric heater actually on the showerhead. They are in common use and good ones work rather well and we had never met anyone who had had an accident with one. Joe fiddled with it and got a proper hot shower.

A change of clothes and refreshed, we looked at our surroundings. A basic room but clean, with the essentials, a bed, an en-suite bathroom, and a covered veranda where we could sip a beer and relax and watch some of the pugnacious hummingbirds searching the flowers in the extensive gardens. In the dining room, where another argumentative parrot kept interrupting the conversation with totally irrelevant remarks, we ate some excellent fish and chips and salad and played dominoes until sleep overcame us.

Chapter 13 The Lower Rio San Juan

It had rained all night and in the morning the Sarapiqui had risen over half a metre. There was a deluge of water pouring into the San Juan and huge tree trunks and debris were tumbling along within it. To our relief, by the time we had finished breakfast the rain had stopped.

We packed the canoe again, thankful that we had lengthened the mooring rope the night before and edged into the Sarapiqui where we sped round a long right hand bend to join the San Juan. The water was boiling in the centre of the river where the main streams from both rivers met, but by keeping close to the bank, we were able to avoid the maelstrom but still had to keep a close look out for floating logs and branches.

The river was wide and curving with islands, most of which were uninhabited and some of which are mini nature reserves. All have names and one is the Isla Nelson. Puttering around one bend a pair of vivid scarlet macaws flew out of the gloomy looking forest and down the river to disappear back into the trees.

Suddenly we came to the entrance of the Rio Colorado, the tremendous river that now takes most of the water of the San Juan out to the Atlantic. We were travelling along the north bank and watched the current with its logs and flower islands spin off down the Colorado. We promised ourselves that one day, we would go down this river to Tortuguero, to watch the turtles coming ashore to lay eggs. A turtle emerging from the sea at night is one of the most amazing ancient sights on earth.

Another check station and 20 cordobas, just over a dollar, for a permit and we are on the last stretch to New Greytown.

Rio San Juan

The river has about 300 islands between the Sarapiqui and New Greytown and their isolation from the forest has made some of them attractive homes to people as there are fewer animals to damage crops. Some of the islands had been used for fortifications and had also provided convenient hiding places for pirates and smugglers. At some places the islands seems to take up the whole river and it was not immediately obvious which route to take around them but by keeping to the widest part of the river, which was now quite placid having lost most of its power to the Colorado, we zig-zagged our way through them. Sometimes logs and branches and floating vegetation had dammed the channel between the forest and the island, sand had collected in the nooks and crannies and the island gradually merged with the riverbank.

There were also sand banks in the river and although we watched out for them, we still got stranded but used the opportunity for a rest and to stretch legs. A small crocodile eyed us from one sand bank but it was more interested in basking in the sun that had, at last, emerged. There were occasional turtles, too, and beaches invaded by stands of cane. In the dry season when the river is lower these beaches and banks are a real problem and even the twice weekly ferry, which knows every twist and turn of the river and keeps a constant check on the water depth, gets stuck, and it is 'everybody out' to push and pull.

The forest is dense with a huge diversity of palms, the familiar coconuts towering high in the sky with their feathery heads. There are Cecropia trees the divided leaves with their characteristic silver undersides shining in the sun, but we see no sloths. There was a myth that 3-toed sloths only ate Cecropia leaves but the reality was that they were just easier to see in a Cecropia tree as the leaves are more widely spaced. We saw no sloths on the entire trip, though that is not to say that no sloth sighted us.

The Cecropia provides food for many birds including the spectacular toucans. We heard their calls but as the binoculars had succumbed to the river water, we now had no way to search for them or any other birds; but it was impossible to miss the shrieking, exotic emerald flocks of parrots.

The Cecropia leaves also provide a breeding ground for the Cecropia Petiole Borer insect, but not any old leaf. The ones that they want have fallen from the tree and caught on something, most likely a branch of another tree, and hang above the ground. The insect then encroaches on the leaf and breeds in the petioles. Up to four pairs may infest one leaf and up to 100 young emerge some 25 days later. They chew into the petiole, pupate and emerge as adults at a staggering size of 2.5 millimetres.

Like other plants in the forest, notably acacias, the Cecropia has resident ants living in the hollow trunk of the tree, which is naturally partitioned into convenient compartments. The ants burrow through the bark and into the trunk where they tend, like cows, their scale insects or mealy bugs. These insects suck the juices from the tree and secrete a fluid containing sugar and several vitamins and amino-acids on which the ants feed. The ants are aggressive in protecting their tree, and the area nearby, and this is very expensive on energy. The sugar mixture is readily available and it offsets some of their calorie loss. The ants are beneficial to the tree by attacking invading insects, notably leaf-cutting ants that can rapidly denude a tree of its leaves, taking them home to their aphid "cows". The Cecropia ant, in return, has a home where, together with its farm animals, has safe housing where it can rear its young in peace.

Rio San Juan

There were fewer river birds here except for a few herons and kingfishers and around one bend we saw a huge bird, a tiger heron, some 80 centimetres tall standing quite motionless and almost hidden with its black, brown and beige barred plumage. We saw two more that morning, all intently staring into the water for food. The river was beginning to turn into a swamp, there were wide areas of weeds, patches of waterlilies and a disturbance in the water. We turned off the engine and espied a crocodile just under the surface, splashing as it made a couple of U turns. Haven't I read somewhere that small engines sound like the territorial calls of other crocodiles? It is not by accident that people are very careful where they swim in this river as, along with the crocodiles, there are many caiman and some of the older people remember incidents with sharks. Thankfully, these crocodiles were nothing like their cousins, the Nile Crocodiles, that used to sunbathe on the beach on the Mara river opposite our house when we lived in Kenya. We could go no further and realised that we had taken a wrong turn. We backed out of the reeds into deeper water and paddled back to the main river, which had made a greater than ninety degree turn that we had completely missed. We turned on the engine and went down to the bar.

Chapter 14 River Squabbles

By the end of the 1700s Granada and San Juan del Norte were beginning to thrive again, both towns expanding and trade increasing. There were additional forts at La Trinidad at the exit of the Sarapiqui river into the San Juan (near to where we had stayed), the isletas near Granada, and at Granada itself. Indians were still raiding and smugglers and pirates were causing problems and the improved forts did little to prevent the attacks and skirmishing. Smuggling was almost a legitimate business with an agent dealing in contraband goods, transactions being conducted in gold dust, doubloons and dollars. The annual trade was worth over 300,000 pesos per annum. Spain was losing its grip and the economy of Nicaragua stagnating and there was pressure and pleading from merchants and landowners for royal permission from Spain to open the lake and river to trade and direct access to Europe, instead of the official route through Guatemala and Hondurus which was long, hazardous and expensive. They also mentioned that Spain could benefit financially if goods went directly into Nicaragua and thence onwards.

Then, revolution and Central America was engaged in the long war of independence from Spain. In Nicaragua it was mainly a guerrilla affair with little in the way of battles though the San Juan was involved in a number of campaigns during which San Carlos was attacked and taken from the Spanish and soon after, by way of the Rio Colorado, the fort at La Trinidad went the same way. There were clashes at San Juan del Norte and trade was disrupted. Eventually on October 3rd 1821 Nicaragua became independent and in 1825 the Central American Federation was formed though it collapsed in 1838 mainly due to Nicaraguan dissention but also political upheaval and revolution. The last to join, it was the first to withdraw. There was an attempt in 1840 to get the federation back together by General Marazon 'The Washington of Central America' but through the conspiracies of foreign agents, Indian mistrust and Catholic meddling, he was expelled and murdered in San Jose in 1842. A quote from a visitor of the time said:

'Nicaragua was formerly the richest state in productions next to San Salvador but is now the most wretched and impoverished of all'.

Sadly, this seems to be a Nicaraguan problem as the same statement could have been made after the Sandanista/Contra war of the 1970s from which Nicaragua has not recovered today. Its markets have gone to other countries and there is continual political squabbling.

Local disagreements between the democrats from Leon, who had taken control of Rivas, and conservatives from Granada led to fighting on the lake and river for control of El Castillo and San Carlos. There was more confusion when the Misquito king granted the lands on both sides of the San Juan river mouth, an area of over 22,500 acres to some US citizens to colonise the area.

During the 1840s San Juan del Norte saw constant claims on its territory. The port was regularly changing hands between the Nicaraguans, British and Misquitos. Even Colombia started concocting a claim. Eventually Britain declared that she was going to restore the town to the Misquito Kingdom. The President seemed resigned to events stating that to protect San Juan del Norte: 'it will be useless and expensive'. On January 1st 1848, with two naval ships and a force of British and Misquito men, San Juan del Norte was taken for the Misquito King, "16 years old and as black as spades", and the town left in the hands of a Misquito governor.

Nicaragua retaliated and General Muñoz was soon off down the river to recover the town. Muñoz returned to Granada leaving his troops at La Trinidad to await British retaliation. They did not have long to wait; on January 24th two hundred or so men in small boats attacked the position and in three hours it was theirs. They continued up the river to take El Castillo and San Carlos where, what became known as the Treaty of the Hundred Islands was signed and Nicaragua recognised Misquito rights at San Juan del Norte.

San Juan del Norte was now in the hands of a British ally, it was recognised by the Nicaraguans and the Misquito flag, with a union jack in the corner, was flying and a direct steamship service between Southampton, England and San Juan del Norte was in operation. Britain agreed to withdraw all her troops, which she honoured, however the name of the town was to be changed to Greytown in honour of Sir Charles Grey the governor of Jamaica who had ordered the San Juan expedition.

The next event that was to dramatically change the status of the river was the California gold rush.

Chapter 15 The Gold Rush and William Walker

Fanciful tales were told of gold to be found in California. Mountain streams 'glowed with reflected light' from the gold flakes lying on the bottom; that Indians would exchange half a pound of gold for a few glass beads. Notwithstanding the more outrageous claims, there was gold and people from the east coast of America were clamouring to get to California by the fastest route possible

To reach California from the eastern United States was extremely difficult. The trails were feint and hazardous, the Indians aggressive; the weather was sometimes appalling and the 'guides', who charged exorbitant amounts of money, guaranteeing to get travellers to their destination, would often just abandon them. The sea route around Cape Horn was equally dangerous and very long.

By 1849 there was a severe shortage of ships for the long trip around the Horn to San Francisco. Any vessel that would float was being consigned to the gold run and, no matter the condition of the ship, they were all full; one had all her berths sold only three hours after they were advertised. Freight-carrying ships were adapted to take passengers and even the New England whaling fleet was taken into service. Comfort was low on the gold miners list of priorities but some of them later regretted that when they were at sea and the hatches were battened down, the temperature freezing and a storm blowing in the Southern Ocean. On a good day they could leave the gloom and emerge on deck to see the sea and the sky and, perhaps, one of the graceful, proud, clippers under full sail. These majestic ships did not get involved in passenger carrying and continued their profitable trading business with China and Indian and other exotic realms. The miner would look with longing, knowing that he was going to take many days longer to reach port, and a few, to never set foot on land again, the ocean taking its toll.

A shorter and quicker route across the Central American isthmus was the answer.

On february 20th 1849, George Gordon with a party of 136 paying passengers left the USA for Greytown in the brig The Mary on the first organised trip across the isthmus. Taking a dismantled steamboat with them, they arrived four weeks later. Greytown was a port town, with all that that implies, and whilst most of the passengers, who were left to guard the luggage and the ship from looters, complained about drunken behaviour, the crew and remaining passengers took to the bars and complained about the lack of food.

The steamer was put together but was either unable to get steam up, or, just did not have enough power to cope with the current and rapids. Eventually she had to be rowed. Consequently, she could only take half the passengers. The rest went up the river in canoes and had a tremendous trip. The others, who had considered themselves lucky to get on the steamer, did not have quite as good a time as it was totally unsuitable for the trip, sandbars had to be negotiated which meant that the ship had to be man-handled around them or even dragged over them. It was hauled over the rapids, sometimes only achieving one ships length every 24 hours. They were running out of food and there were no farms. They were terrified of the jungle but discovered that iguanas were easy to catch and good to eat, crocodile eggs could be collected, and crocodiles themselves killed and eaten, whilst birds made good soup and the river had plenty of fish. One day they caught a 100lb shark and on the menu that night was fried alligator tail, shark chowder and stewed monkey. Twenty-one days after leaving Greytown they reached San Carlos. There they ate another meal and, still complaining about lack of food (though they seem to have found plenty), they left for a rough lake crossing to Granada where:

'upwards of five hundred of the citizens of Granada assembled on the beach to receive and welcome (them) with enthusiastic shouts'.

It was July 20th before they left for San Francisco. Along with tales of their drunken fights and brawls, all they left behind was an American flag on the top of Mombacho, some graffiti on the walls of El Castillo and a clutch of surprisingly pale skinned babies. Squier, the official American representative of the government was sent to Nicaragua in 1849 and arrived a few days later after a three-hour trip up the rapids, even though his bongo was not carrying any freight, where he saw a few thatched houses and the fort. He climbed to the castle and crossed the fosse into its two floors of chambers sunk into the rock and along the bombproof passage into the chapel. He noticed the grafitti on the walls and back in town:

'a pretty girl in a hammock calls out 'adios California', one naked leg hanging indolently over the side as she threw aside her long black curls. Clearly she was on familiar terms with the group of rowdy Californians that had passed through a few days earlier.'

The river now went big-time. Cornelius Vanderbilt wanted to expand his shipping empire and was fascinated by the idea of an isthmus route, even a canal, and in 1849 managed to get a charter from the Nicaraguan government that gave his new Atlantic and Pacific Ship Canal Company exclusive rights to get from one ocean to the other by any route it wanted. January 21st 1850 the first ship, the 250 ton

Orus, arrived. She was not really suitable for the river but by using the Rio Colorado made her way to the San Juan and reached the Machuca rapids. Then the Director arrived, a shallow draft 120 ton double side-wheeler, she had travelled all the way up the San Juan and joined the Orus To try to create an easier passage, rocks had been dynamited in the Machuca rapids for weeks, but on her attempt to get through, the Orus was swept away, too badly damaged ever to be used again. The Director reached El Castillo where there had been more dynamiting of rocks in the El Diablo rapids and, eventually, she was pulled by ropes through the rapids to arrive in Granada almost one year after leaving Greytown and made history as the first steamship to navigate the isthmus waterway from Greytown to Granada.

Vanderbilt, himself, arrived shortly after at San Carlos in the Prometheus, which was pulling the Sir Henry Bulwer that had been especially built for the San Juan and was to be used to search for the best land route from the lake to the Pacific. He eventually decided on the short route from La Virgen to San Juan del Sur.

This new route was welcomed and newspaper articles sang its praises. It was shorter, there were only 12 miles of land to cross, the climate was cooler and there was less disease. Not all these claims were entirely true and there were plenty of complaints from early passengers about oppressive heat during the day and swarms of insects at night and malaria, cholera and yellow fever.

No matter the discomfort and the route barely tested, Vanderbilt had more passengers than he could manage and many had to endure long delays. Some of the newspaper articles back home began to take on a less enthusiastic tone with a series of letters for and against the route. One letter, by a Dr. Rabe written in 1851, that initiated an outburst of rebuttals, is worth quoting.

'I was a passenger on the Prometheus, from New York, July 14th last. We reached San Juan del Norte on the 23rd; left there by the iron steamer, Sir Henry L. Bulwer, on the 24th; ran about 45 miles up the San Juan River; and came to anchor for the night. On the 26th, having walked around the portage (300 yards) we took bungos, ten miles to the Toro rapid, where we got on board the steamer Director, for Virgin Bay; arrived there at daylight Sunday, 27th, but finding no signal of the arrival of the steamship Pacific at San Juan del Sur, we passed up the lake ten miles, to the city of Rivas, a place of 10,000 inhabitants, where we remained until Thursday, and then came on board the Pacific; left San Juan on Friday, at 2 P.M.....Hereafter the ships and boats will meet regularly, and the passengers will pass over the Company's road to Virgin Bay, (12 miles and 18 chains) which it is true, is now only a mule road, but it is being laid with plank, and will soon be a good wagon road. However, with all the obstacles incident to a first trip, I came from ocean to ocean, in exactly 40 hours running time...'

The main objection was that it may have been 40 hours running time, but it actually took 5 days.

The planking was put down and shortly after, blue and white stagecoaches and wagons were using the land section. It was along this stretch of road that Mark Twain in 1866 was less than enthusiastic about the advertising efforts of enterprising Yankees.

'There was some round abuse indulged in...of...such people, who invade all places with their rascally signs, and mar every landscape one might gaze upon in worship...'

Business boomed but Nicaraguans were feeling that they were not getting enough from all the traffic and that the money was all going into the pockets of foreigners. Tensions were already strained between the Ship Canal Company and the port authorities at Greytown as ships were refusing to pay port taxes. The Ship Canal Company was against the recently negotiated Clayton-Bulwer treaty that declared Greytown a freeport, so the company upped and moved to the opposite side of the harbour to Punta Arenas, built new offices and warehouses, leaving Greytown much less well-off. By 1854 there was more business than ships and half the people travelling the isthmus were using this route, but Nicaragua was again fighting amongst itself.

The internal situation was one of turmoil and barbarous disputes, cruel and savage conflicts between Indian tribes, Negroes and Whites that resulted in carnage. The conservatives and democrats were vying for power and there had been fifteen presidents in the last six years. Chamorro for the conservatives was a rich, pompous, aristocrat seeking absolute power whilst his opposer, Castellon, was looking for a power base amongst the poor and less privileged. Although neither had a clear majority, Chamorro claimed the presidency, cast Castellon and some of his supporters into prison and fettered the Supreme Court. This suppression of any opposition and justice galvanised the country and the democratic cause grew and flowered into full-scale political resistance. Castellon and friends were banished as 'dangerous to the peace of the land' and retreated to Honduras. There they gathered support and vowed to free Nicaragua from its "aristocratic tyrants". They marched to León, success all the way, and drove Chamorro to Granada.

But, the promises they had made were impossible to fulfil and their supporters became disenchanted with the lack of progress.

Meanwhile, in Granada, Chamorro had welcomed the support and influence of the Catholic Church so Castellon declared a siege on Granada to try to get rid of him. It lasted nine months during which time Chamorro died and the whole episode only led to yet another period of quarrelsome, bloody, fighting.

The Ship Canal Company was making big profits but Vanderbilt was again refusing to pay taxes, this time his Nicaraguan taxes, claiming, with some justification, that the internal confusion make it impossible to know to whom to pay them. There was skirmishing on the river and the liberals eventually took over the abandoned forts at San Carlos and El Castillo.

In Greytown, where tempers were getting short, mainly due to the transit company's refusal to comply with the terms agreed with the town's authorities, news of an incident on the river reached the town. A steamboat had collided with a small Nicaraguan boat and, after a shouting match between the Nicaraguan, Antonio Paladino a Negro citizen of Greytown, and the ship's captain, Captain Smith, Smith took out his gun, aimed, fired and killed the inoffensive Nicaraguan. The people of Greytown wanted to arrest Smith and a mob gathered outside the US Consul's residence where he had taken refuge, but the Americans refused to give him up. During the fracas a bottle was thrown cutting the cheek of a US official who then demanded $24,000 compensation and that the perpetrator be punished. The US Minister to Central America, Borland, who had been on Smith's ship at the time of the outrage and who was now staying with the Consul, was temporarily held hostage but eventually allowed to board a ship back to New York. Two days later a British ship steamed into the harbour and peace was restored.

Borland, now back in Washington, demanded that a sloop be sent down to Greytown to support the transit company and protect its rights and its refusal to pay passenger taxes. On its arrival at Greytown a message was sent ashore to say that the town was going to be shelled and everyone should move to the safety of Punta Arenas. At 9.00 am on a July morning in 1854 Greytown was destroyed and 35 marines sent ashore to finish the job by burning what was left. In the end this proved more of an annoyance than a catastrophe as the town was re-built almost immediately.

The conservatives now set forth from Granada to re-take the waterway with three ships that they had had re-fitted and another three that they had captured on the lake. They proceeded to overrun San Carlos and El Castillo with a toll of 50 democrats dead and two conservatives. Rivas, near the land isthmus was taken and the waterway was once again secured for the conservatives.

The democrats now needed help, and deliverance came in the unlikely guise of three men, one of whom was Byron Cole, who left San Francisco in 1854 to develop commercial trade between the United States and Central American countries and expand the gold mines about which they were sure they had reliable, valuable, information.

They made their way to León and the democrat party headquarters where they were welcomed and dined. It was clear to Cole that in order to achieve peace after 25 years of armed squabbles between León and Granada, and a deeply divided country that the democrats needed experienced soldiers. Cole was a friend and business associate of William Walker and he suggested to Castellon that he send for:

'...the renowned Walker' whom he described as:

'...one of the bravest and most capable of American adventurers and ready at all times to enter into negotiations to enlist with his friends in matters relating to the Spanish American Republic'.

An agreement was made whereby, if Cole with Walker would support the democratic cause, they would receive 21,000 acres of land.

Cole returned to San Francisco and found Walker editing The State Journal. He explained the situation to him and the arrangement he had entered into but Walker rejected the terms as he thought that the reward was not high enough to compensate for the very real risks involved. However, if the land grant was increased to 52,000 acres, he would agree to the terms and go to the democrats aid.

Back in León, the new terms were agreed and Walker raised money and men.

The history of Walker in Nicaragua has had different interpretations but it is agreed that he went to Nicaragua at the express request of one of the most important men in the country. Nicaragua had very little going for it but Walker realised immediately that this might be just the opportunity he needed to bring to fruition his long-held dream of establishing an American colony, an Anglican slave state in a Central American country with all the land owned by whites. He had already failed in a disastrous incursion to take over the Sonora in Mexico and Nicaragua might be exactly what he wanted.

Walker was a lawyer-doctor-journalist from Nashville, Tennessee; a man about whom most Americans know nothing whilst in Nicaragua, he is a household name. In appearance he was quite unprepossessing, 5 feet 4 inches tall, slender with a long face but full, rather coarse lips, a pale complexion and very light close-cropped hair over a broad rounded forehead. He struck one as a thoughtful, serious man who rarely smiled but whose main feature were spell-binding deep blue-grey eyes that were to become famous.

His father was a Scottish banker who emigrated as a rich man to the United States around 1820 and William was born in 1824. He had a strict up-bringing and a good classical education. He became a lawyer and moved to New Orleans. Later he studied medicine in Philadelphia and spent a year in Europe before returning to New Orleans. Walker had little to do with women in his life but when he was leaving Paris he wrote a poem that gives a glimpse of a perturbed mind with a chilling vision of what his future might be.

'My desperate heart runs from one to another,
who knows if I shall live to be thirty,
whether the future will be gay,
or whether I shall be shot,
only kiss me Camille, kiss me.'

He did, however, meet and fall in love with an extremely beautiful woman, Helen Martin, who was both deaf and dumb. A wedding day was fixed but before the marriage she died of yellow fever. Walker was completely shattered by her death, never got over the loss and took to his grave the jeweled cross that she had given him.

Walker then turned to journalism and followed the Gold Rush to California and joined The Herald newspaper.

There, his forthright style and acerbity led to jail and a $500 fine for contempt of court though crowds of his readers protested in the streets against his sentence. He then switched back to law and became financially very successful though he was totally indifferent to wealth or personal luxury.

Walker met much opposition and disapproval when it was known that he was getting involved in Central America again. He was jeered by the press and sneered at by politicians and capitalists but on the 4th May 1855 in a small brig, The Vesta, he sailed with 57 men, filibusters, armed with rifles, revolvers and bowie knives. The ship was under an attachment order and earlier that day Walker had persuaded the deputy sheriff to come aboard and inspect some papers that he had. Once on board Walker courteously invited him to step below for some refreshment where he then informed him that he was sailing that night, but that if he offered no resistance there would be no violence. The ship sailed, the deputy sheriff, after arranging for a tug to assist them out of the harbour, quaffed champagne and smoked a cigar until he was returned to land in the tug.

The term filibuster is defined as a person who outfits at private expense a body of armed men for operations in a foreign country with which his country is at peace. This was exactly the situation when Walker was gathering his troops to fight in Nicaragua and there seems little argument that he was indeed a filibuster.

The Vesta arrived in Corinto on the Pacific coast in June 1855 and Walker headed down to León. A close friend of his, Capt. C.W. Doubleday, wrote that Walker had said that he felt that his arrival in Nicaragua was the first step in his conquest of the country.

'To make himself emperor of a mighty slave-holding empire stretching from Texas to the Isthmus of Panama.'

Of these thoughts, Castellon knew nothing.

Walker was at the head of his troops, a rather unimpressive figure but with his troops marching into town in open-necked blue flannel shirts, knee-high leather boots, felt hats cocked, rifles shining, 'colts swaying on slender hips' and drums beating, they may not have been exactly in step but they were a swaggering band of some of the finest fighting men in the world.

It was soon after his arrival that Walker met with a group of Indians and heard, for the first time the prophesy that, after many years of misery, their people would be freed by a stranger from the north 'a grey-eyed man of destiny'. A prophecy that apparently deeply moved him and which would follow him for the rest of his life.

Walker had learnt that the democrats were not doing well, news with which he was quite content as he thought it would make him more welcome and indeed when he arrived at León he and his men were all given Nicaraguan citizenship and were enlisted into the Nicaraguan army. Walker was given the rank of Colonel with Muñoz as the Commanding General of the army. Muñoz was opposed to the filibusters and in his blue uniform with red lining with plenty of gilt, Walker took an instant dislike to him, distrusted him and he refused to fight under him. He had quickly made a powerful enemy.

On learning of the situation in Nicaragua it quickly became clear to him that if he was going to get anywhere he had to get control of the waterway, the transit road and Rivas to solve the problem of how to supply his troops and how to get more of his filibusters into the country. Muñoz was against any operation of this kind but he was over-ruled by Castellon so Walker, his men, and 100 of Castellon's troops left León for an early and unprepared foray on Rivas. To surprise the garrison there they marched through jungle mud for two days and nights in torrential rain, his guides lost. When the rain stopped, Walker was awed by the forest, the birds, the huge butterflies, macaws, the noise of a million cicadas, wide columns of ants and the air, perfumed by flowers an experience that stayed with him.

At Tola, en route to Rivas, they encountered 20 conservative troops who immediately raced to Rivas with the news that Walker was on his way and where the town prepared and waited. The odds were greatly in the conservatives favour particularly as Castellon's men had fled into the forest and Walker was left with his 57. The battle of Rivas was fierce and bitter, the house which Walker's men had taken as a base was burnt and they had to resort to hand to hand fighting to escape from the town. Although easily beaten with ten of his men killed, including his two commanders, and twelve injured, the opposition sustained 180 men killed or injured. Walker had lost this ill-prepared battle but it gave him and his men a well-earned reputation for skill and bravery that would stand them in good stead for future conflicts.

Walker called Castellon's troops cowards, and Muñoz a traitor as he believed that Muñoz had leaked the plan of attack to the conservatives and when he was killed soon after, in battle, many believed that he had been assassinated by an agent of Walker's.

Walker was now asked to take and occupy southern Nicaragua by Castellon and the water route was seen as the best way to achieve this. Around September 1855 a notoriously cruel professional revolutionary and supporter of the conservatives, Gardiola, arrived in Nicaragua from Honduras and appeared at Rivas. Walker with his men and 120 natives set out for La Virgen, the start of the land route to the Pacific and in conservative hands. Gardiola, followed behind. Along the way, Walker was surprised and fired on by a party of 100 conservatives marching along the transit road to La Virgen. After Walker reached La Virgen he ended up with his back to the lake and Gardiola attacking from all three sides. He had his troops deployed in three groups but knew that he could expect no quarter from Gardiola, the fight would be to the death. The bravery of Walker and his 170 men was admirable and eventually Gardiola retreated leaving 60 dead. Walker was a minor casualty of this battle when he was hit in the neck by a spent ball. Many of the enemy came over to Walker's side whilst others fled into the hills and forests leaving over 400 precious muskets behind. Walker had the transit road but Castellon died of cholera before learning of the victory.

Walker's eyes were now firmly set on Granada but whilst waiting for reinforcements all plans had to be put on hold when the hidden enemy, cholera, appeared in El Castillo. The fort was so badly affected that, in order to protect his property, Vanderbilt had to put his own men into the fort to keep control. The cholera quickly spread and the death rate was high, over 600 dead in León and Granada was left seriously undermanned. A shipload of men had arrived from California to support Walker and now was the time to attack.

When La Virgen anchored in Virgen bay, Walker and his men commandeered the ship and set steam for Granada. The night was very dark and rain threatening when, with all lights extinguished, she dropped anchor about three miles from Granada. By 3.00am all the troops were ashore and in single file, Walker with them, they trudged along a muddy trail, picking their way through the undergrowth and into Granada with its garrison of 400 and population of 8,000. The town was unprepared and they met little resistance but 16 men were killed, only one of who was Walker's; by lunchtime, Granada was theirs.

At the San Francisco church they were appalled to find 80 prisoners, men, women and children, all in chains and in terrible conditions. All were released. The fort was captured and then the Gran Plaza. Nearly 400 prisoners were taken but Walker prevented the execution of the conservative officials and forbade pillage and disorder. Walker was no longer a petty adventurer, he was seen as a liberator and although a strict disciplinarian he did not torture and rarely ordered executions.

The conservative, General Corral, was in charge in Rivas and Walker had, obviously, not told him of his designs on Granada. The United States minister, John Wheeler, resident in Granada agreed to act as part of the commission to negotiate peace terms but wanted to wait for Corral. Corral was furious, resented Wheeler's involvement and refused to negotiate with Walker on any terms whatsoever. The democrats now held the conservative capital, Granada, but the conservatives still had Rivas and controlled the water route.

Granada was a sophisticated town, the market sold cottons from England, silk and wine from France, jewellery from Spain and each year many of the wealthy Granadanians would travel to Europe for pleasure, sight-seeing or to study. There was music in the town, horse parades and dancing. Nina Yrena (or Irena Ohoran) was a middle-aged woman of Irish descent with a house in Granada that was a 'salon' for the most influential aristocrats, all conservatives, in the town. Walker told her that she would be his hostess for as long as he desired, effectively stopping the plotting in one step. Other sources say that she invited him to stay at her house, perhaps to keep an eye on him for her friends. She did teach him about the complexities of Nicaraguan politics but was probably not Walker's mistress, although there was plenty of gossip in the town, as she already had a high-ranking lover, Espinosa, who Walker described as 'a man without principle and without humour'. an Walker later accused him of plotting against him and had him deported, which rather cooled his relationship with Doña Ohoran.

Whilst all this was going on, passengers were coming and going from New York to California. Amongst one of these groups were 60 mercenaries arriving to aid Walker. Instead of going straight to Granada and checking in with Walker, they went to La Virgen and commandeered a boat, the La Virgen, together with the passengers onboard, and attempted to take San Carlos. San Carlos had been forewarned, ignored a request for them to surrender, and promptly opened fire on the ship, which retreated to Granada, where the mercenaries were landed. The unfortunate passengers were then taken back to La Virgen and the transit company building, to await transport for the land trip to San Juan del Sur on the Pacific.

At this point a misunderstanding occurred. The towns of La Virgen and Granada were in democrat hands. The mercenaries had attempted to take San Carlos in La Virgen, the transit company owned ship that had been involved in the taking of Granada and La Virgen. Consequently, the conservatives thought that the transit company had done a deal with the democrats and that all the ships were in democrat hands.

Conservative forces entered the town of La Virgen to find the filibusters (who were all in Granada) when from somewhere shots were fired. The conservative captain thought that the shots had come from the transit building and, in the ensuing chaos fired on the transit building with the 250 innocent, unfortunate, passengers inside, leaving three dead and others wounded. Many of the passengers had fled into the forest when the horsemen entered the town but when neither Walker nor or any of his filibusters were found, free passage was offered to the passengers.

To really confuse the situation, the ship San Carlos was heading for San Carlos with a group of passengers that it had picked up above the El Toro rapids. Although the San Carlos, together with all the other ships on the river was armed, the fort was jittery and fearful of another attack and the garrison, mistakenly thinking that the ship was now a democrat vessel and, possibly, carrying filibusters, fired on the San Carlos. A 24lb shot (or 18lb depending on the source) screamed through the side of the ship killing Mrs Alexander White of Clinton, California and one of her children whilst another was fatally injured and died five hours later having had both legs shot off. All were buried in San Carlos. The astonished, crippled, ship veered off to La Virgen completely unaware of what had provoked the attack.

The La Virgen and the San Carlos met somewhere in the lake and exchanged gossip about their experiences and jointly decided that the waterway was too dangerous. All the passengers from the San Carlos were transferred to the La Virgen, which had already taken on board the passengers from the transit building. There were now 400 people on the ship, many of them wounded, or suffering from cholera, and she left for the hospital at Omotepe. But Omotepe was now in conservative hands and they too were prepared to fire on, what they thought was a democrat ship. The La Virgen was in a really desperate state, overcrowded, with food shortages and no medicines or dressings. She dared not call in at any port for fear of being fired upon and could not land passengers at Granada as it was in the throws of a cholera epidemic and, fuel was low. Passengers were dying at such a rate that, eventually, they were unceremoniously thrown overboard for the sharks, with no attempt at funeral services. Eventually she limped towards Granada where she managed to get a load of wood on her third night and left for San Jorge, near La Virgen.

Walker needed to retain control of the transit route and Granada and not have them revert to conservative control once he left the town. The chaos, misunderstandings, blunders and action on the lake played straight into democrat and Walker's hands. What he did, however, was uncharacteristic and against his stated beliefs. He was holding prisoner Mateo Mayoraga, the most prominent legitimist politician and Walker ordered him shot, even though, as he well knew, he was completely innocent of any involvement with the events at La Virgen.

When news of this reached General Corral and other conservatives, who all had friends, relatives and property in Granada that they wanted to protect, they called for peace and on the 23rd October 1855 terms were agreed. Patricio Rivas, a moderate conservative was President and Walker, who held the real power, was elected Commander in Chief of the Army.

Sixteen days after Walker entered Granada there was peace, and a new government, one with a majority of Walker's supporters in the cabinet. Walker immediately put his troops along the waterway at La Virgen, San Carlos and El Castillo. He wanted to tighten his control and start his treasured idea of an American colony and promote American and European immigration; single men to receive 250 acres of land and families, 350 acres. He also sought a country based on justice and without corruption.

Things were looking good for Walker, but there were problems downriver. Settlers had arrived to take up the offer of land made by the Misquitos near Greytown and these included Kinney who came to take possession of the 'kingdom' and with great aplomb even started a newspaper. The settlers however, after getting no support from anyone and disease taking its inevitable toll, mostly left. Some travelled inland to join Walker, including Kinney who arrived carrying a muddled proposal for Walker, but Walker made it quite clear that he had absolutely no time for him. A comment by Walker made around that time made it quite clear that his policy, from the very beginning, was to claim and hold for Nicaragua her entire territory from ocean to ocean and set aside all:

'Mosquito coasts, Kinney kingdoms, Samba rights and British Protectorates'.

Everything, however, took a different turn on November 5th when Walker was shown a letter that had been intercepted which had been sent from General Corral to Gardiola, who was now back in Honduras. It talked about the expulsion of the Americans and their destruction. That he was against the government and was calling for assistance from other Central American countries; it was treasonable. Corral was arrested and sentenced to be shot but the court unanimously recommended mercy. Corral was popular and when Walker went ahead with the execution the people turned away from him and the foreign members of their government. Walker justified his action as upholding his new treaty and that a pardon would not have set right 'an injustice to many'.

Walker still had everything going his way and by the 1st March 1856 he had 1,200 men deployed around the country. He had passed numerous decrees to restore order and guarantee the safety of life and property and to open up the magnificent resources of the country. He gave immunity to political offenders and invited fugitives to return. He made English the official language, started a newspaper, El Nicaraguense, and sent promotional information to the United States to encourage ranchers, farmers, miners, scientists and businessmen to come and settle. Besides the inducements of land, some of which had been confiscated from the 'enemies of the state' Walker was honest in his descriptions of the richness of the agriculture, of the fruits that could be grown including oranges, lemons, limes, bananas, papayas, cocoa, avocado, guava, plantains, granadillos and melons and as he was genuinely captivated by the scenery, the lakes and forests and the volcanoes.. He told of sugar, tobacco, coffee, indigo, corn, rice, chocolate and hardwood trees. That there was gold, silver, copper and other minerals, fields for cattle and an abundance of fish and shellfish. And, there was cheap labour, particularly as he had repealed Nicaragua's anti-slavery law.

About 1,000 people flocked to Nicaragua from the southern states and California from all classes of society in the following year. Many were miners; seduced by the lure of gold in California they had ended up worse off than they were before they had left their homes and Walker's call for armed men and immigrants with a promise of land was enticing. When the Uncle Sam sailed from California her decks were thronged with nearly 300 men with their carpet-bags and blankets and filibusters with arms. An equal number were left on the docks, no room on the ship.

By 1856 the lake was seething with ships. Two schooners were calling into ports around the lake, there were some twelve steamships, twenty-nine launches, and various lighters, yawls and canoes. There were railroads around rapids, warehouses, workshops and boat builders, and money was being made.

Walker wanted the transit route. He was arrogant, had already made errors and enemies, and when he saw what he thought was an opportunity, he made a tremendous mistake. The transit route charter had been granted to Vanderbilt with a franchise, held by two companies, to build a canal to join the two oceans. Walker persuaded two friends in San Franciso to enter into a conspiracy and, representing a new company, they declared the existing charter forfeit and that all its property should be seized as the francise owed money and no canal had been built. Vanderbilt's accountants had probably massaged the accounts but it was still completely unjustifiable and illegal, as Walker knew very well. He saw it as a shortcut to his own power and self-aggrandizement. Rivas, very reluctantly, signed the new charter.

Vanderbilt was a rich, tobacco-chewing ungrammatical and profane man whose passion was money.

'What do I care about the law. Hain't I got the power.'

He had recently shipped 250 recruits, at his own expense, to join Walker and thought that Walker was a friend but he was unable to come to any satisfactory arrangement with him. Vanderbilt then stopped all the transit route traffic reportedly saying:

'I won't sue you for the law is too slow, I will ruin you'.

He owned all the ships and stopped them all from leaving New York and California with the result that the passenger trade came to a complete standstill, together with all its revenues and Walker had no way to get his filibusters to Nicaragua.

Costa Rica was Walker's next problem as it was threatening the waterway and although he tried to settle the matter diplomatically, the talks failed and Costa Rica declared war. Led by General Mora, the Costa Ricans raised the black flag, a declaration that all prisoners taken with arms would be shot.

Walker chose Rivas for his base and had set up his headquarters by the 1st April. Although he had 1,200 Americans under his command, he had not received any new recruits since Vanderbilt had halted his ships and those he had, had to be spread along the river and enough kept in Granada to protect that town

. By the 8th April, Walker was back in Granada. Mora saw this as a golden opportunity to take the transit route and immediately moved; he took Santa Rosa on the way, in Costa Rican hands to this day, and continued on to La Virgen where his troops fired on transit company labourers and killed nine. They broke open and looted the company building and burned the $120,000 wharf before continuing on to Rivas.

Walker learned of the raid and next day, although he was very ill, took the road to Rivas with 550 Americans and camped nine miles from Rivas where some 2,700 troops faced him. On the 11th April, to the surprise of the Costa Ricans, Walker attacked the town. The attack was well-planned and the Costa Ricans disorganised but they had taken refuge in the western area of town where, with no artillery, it was difficult for Walker's men to penetrate the barricades. The battle was fierce with as many as 30 guns firing at once along with rifles and revolvers. It was long and hard with much damage, and much bravery from Walker and his men. More than 600 Costa Ricans were killed; 58 Americans were dead and 62 wounded. Walker retreated to Granada, where he then had to squash a conservative rebellion against the government. Then cholera, this time in

Rivas, came to his aid as it devastated the Costa Rican troops and led to their withdrawal from most of Nicaragua and Walker was able to regain control.

Walker was wearing out his welcome with his Nicaraguan friends as they were beginning to understand his alternative agenda. When Castellon invited Walker and his men to Nicaragua it was as a filibuster force, to help him gain political power for himself and his party and oust the conservatives. The payment of money and land was solely meant as remuneration for this purpose, not as a basis for colonisation. Walker had never had any thoughts of defending the weak and oppressed against the rich; he wanted to overthrow the existing social conditions and end the chaos in the country to create a modern, successful, industrial system and he had the man-power to do it

'the native Indian would prove the full equal of the Negro as slave'.

Walker's stance on slavery is extremely unclear. Nowhere does he say that slaves can be 'owned' but he refers to the Indians as potential slaves and with an assumption that the Indians would be used as the work force. He also considered that the status of slave might be a step up for some of the very poorest Nicaraguans. His repeal of the anti-slavery law was seen as just one of a batch of laws that he repealed and which had no particular significance; whilst others declared that he had a desire to turn Nicaragua into a southern slave state of the United States with slavery at its core and Walker at its head, the slave idea a lure to get southern farmers to Nicaragua.

Patricio Rivas denounced him as dangerous to Nicaragua, stripped him of his rank, and his position in government. Completely undismayed by Rivas's actions, Walker marched out of Rivas to Granada, pipe and drums playing, and managed to get himself elected as President even though there were two other claimants, Rivas and Estrada in Granada. He was installed on July 12th 1856 declaring that he was the choice of the people. Both the conservatives and democrats were outraged by this turn of events and united to rid themselves and Nicaragua of Walker. Britain was also against Walker as they saw him as helping American expansionism and a threat to their own Misquito Coast protectorate so they supplied Costa Rica with the arms to fight against him. As well as the help from Costa Rica in the south, help was also forthcoming for the coalition from Guatemala in the north. The National War commenced.

Walker prepared for the Costa Rican invasion by moving to La Virgen in the ship San Carlos with his filibuster troops, the only men still supporting him. He sent men to protect the transit route, amongst them an explosives expert, Frederick Henningsen. Of Swedish stock he had been born in England, was handsome and amusing and had written books about his adventures and campaigns in Spain, Hungary and Russia. He was married to a southern beauty and reached Granada in October 1856 when he was 42 years old. He was, by far, Walker's best officer and was headquartered in the Convent San Francisco in Granada. The Costa Ricans knew that Walker's strength lay in the waterway and they planned an attack from the Pacific at San Juan del Sur to take the isthmus land route. Granada had been left in the hands of Henningsen. Walker, aware of everything that was happening against him, ordered Henningsen to burn Granada.

The two steamships La Virgen and San Carlos started a shuttle service to carry men, women and children, the sick and wounded, their armaments and valuables to Omotepe.

Rio San Juan

Five days later Henningsen was starting to set the fires when conservative troops arrived. Had Henningsen's men not resorted to looting and not been drunk, they would all have been long gone. As it was, the La Virgen had taken on the last of the goods and, as it did not have enough fire power to protect itself, untied and steamed into the lake, abandoning 27 men in the process at the small lakeside fort, and headed for Walker at La Virgen to tell him what was going on. Walker left for Granada where he found the men left at the fort on the lake. They seemed to be in good straits so he provisioned them and instructed them to keep the route from the town to the lake open for Henningsen and his men. But, one of these men, possibly a filibuster who could see he was on the wrong side or, more likely, one of the political prisoners that Walker had released, went to the conservative garrison which, on being told of the small number of men in the fort, attacked and killed all but one who swam out to Walker in the San Carlos with the news.

Henningsen had known that Granada might be attacked but he mistook the shots in the night as coming from Walker's men. It was only in the morning that he realised that the lake outpost had been overrun and that he was caught in the centre of the city with about 300 men, some wounded, and 70 women, children and sick. There was fighting in the town and the Guadalupe church was lost. Situated on the outskirts of Granada on the road to the lake, its loss effectively cut off Henningsen's escape route. He was now getting into a desperate situation, short of food, with sick and injured soldiers and civilians. He tried to re-take the church and failed but then in a state of sheer desperation, he and his men bombarded and rushed it, took it and had a sanctuary. The conditions in the church were appalling, injured and sick were lying side by side, the only food, a little mule meat, no sanitation or medical care. There were corpses lying in the streets and the stench of bodies decomposing in the heat and sun, overpowering. It took them 3 days to fight their way out of town and down to the lake, burning the town as they went.

Walker took his time; he was steaming back and forth between La Virgen, which feared an attack from Costa Rican troops, Omotepe where the Indians were revolting and, keeping an eye on Granada. It was more than two weeks before he was back at anchor off Granada with new recruits when he received a note from Henningsen. This note had been brought to him by one of Henningsen's men swimming out to his ship with the note enclosed in a bottle, and it gave some suggestions for signals if Walker was going to rescue them. Receipt of the note was acknowledged by the wave of a hat from a seaman rowed inshore and, during that next dark and windy night, Walker's filibusters rowed ashore to exactly the same spot where they had originally landed to take Granada, and headed for the town. A couple of skirmishes and Henningsen and his men, what were left of them as by now many had died of their injuries, disease and hunger, were rescued from the smouldering remains of Granada. By the end of those three weeks in Granada, 124 were killed or wounded, 120 had died of cholera, 40 had deserted and 2 taken prisoner.

There were 111 armed men left from a force of 277. Before leaving Henningsen made a flag from a piece of partly burnt rawhide, used a charred stick as a pencil and a shattered lance as a pole and stuck it in the ground near the blackened Guadalupe church. The sign, which made him famous, declared:

'Aqui fue Granada' (here was Granada).

Chapter 16 Omotepe

Omotepe has been called 'The Island of Peace' and the name has stuck. Except when used by pirates for some rest, recreation, food and women after looting and pillaging in Granada, it was a place of refuge, a safe haven. Somehow the island managed to avoid nearly all the fighting that occurred on the lake and in the towns around it, even during the Sandanista/Contra war of recent history.

Once there was no lake Cocibolca, just a fruitful verdant valley with birds and deer. It belonged to the gods and Coapol was charged with caring for the valley. Some Indian tribes lived around the edge and they fought amongst themselves . One day the beautiful Ometepetl from the Nicaragua tribe and the handsome warrior Nagrando from the Chorotega tribe met and fell in love. But their tribes were enemies and marriage between the two tribes was forbidden. The two lovers were seen together and Ometepetl's father swore that he would kill Nagrando but they escaped into the forest where the gods married them in life and afterlife. They realised that there was no hope for them in this life so they vowed to die rather than live apart, so amongst the beauty of the valley, they cut their wrists. The skies became dark, thunder roared, lightening flashed and a meteorite shot across the sky. There was a torrential downpour of rain that filled the valley with water. As death overcame them Nagrando stumbled away and fell, his body to become Zapatera (the shape of a man's body can be imagined) while Omatopetl became Omatepe, her breasts swelling above the waters. The people of their tribes were drowned and formed the Isletas of Granada and the Solentiname islands.

Omotepe is staggeringly beautiful and lies in the middle of Lake Cocibolca. Two perfect conical volcanoes joined by a five kilometre stretch of lava. Concepción, one of the world's most symmetrical volcanoes is 1,610 metres high. An active volcano thought to be dormant when first discovered, she leapt into life in 1838 and has erupted, irregularly, ever since, a plume of gas always drifting from her summit, just to remind you. We could just see Concepción from our house but our early warning system, a pair of binoculars, may not have been very effective. Plans to evacuate Omotepe have been made should a serious threat of an eruption occur but the last time that the islanders were asked to leave many refused, saying that they would rather die than leave the island. The second volcano, Maderas, is smaller at 1,394 metres and sleeping with a mysterious misty crater lake that was only discovered by outside people in 1930.

The volcanoes of Omotepe are today, still covered in forests, and waterfalls cascade. Fruits and flowers abound and brightly coloured birds and huge butterflies fly amongst the trees. There are thousands of parakeets and many howler monkeys, their calls echoing. It is the ultimate tropical romantic paradise. But there is something strange about the forests; those on Concepción are dry tropical forests with the beautiful guanacaste trees whilst those on Madera are wet lush jungle with even an elfin forest towards the top, something out of Lord of the Rings. That these two volcanoes have such different ecological systems in such a small area is very strange but greatly increases the diversity of life found there.

This island needs protection and it is found in the form of Chico Verde a descendent of chief Nicarao who was buried with his treasure near Charco Verde, a remote spot on Omotepe. Chico Verde guards the tomb but in addition (he probably didn't have enough to do and was looking for something interesting, stimulating and worthwhile) he decided that he would guard all the island's wildlife and the fish, some 35 species, which he does to this day but he could certainly do with some extra help regarding the fish.

To escape the bloody Aztec tribes of Mexico, the Chorotega and Nicorao tribes fled south. The Chorotega's were the first to arrive around 1,200 AD and legend has it that they were guided by a prophecy that they would find a land next to a great lake with two volcanoes. When they reached the great lake, there they settled alongside the existing tribes. They gave the land the name Nic-Anahuac 'here arrived those of the Anahuac' and later Spanish mispronunciation gave us Nicaragua. They called the lake Coatpolcan corrupted by the Spanish into Cocibolca. They came with their gods too, gods of fertility, of the earth, the air and death. They believed in an afterlife and thought that natural disasters were inevitable and stored food and water for any next event. They had a calender of 360 days and left pottery, statues and stone carvings. However, Omotepe has been inhabited for a very long time and there are occasional glimpses of a civilization much older, part of the mysteriousness and magic that is Omotepe.

In 1872, accompanying a US Navy expedition to Nicaragua and Costa Rica that was charged with making a survey for an inter-oceanic ship canal, was a medical officer, J.F. Bransford. During this trip and two subsequent ones he spent much time on Omotepe and found an agricultural community growing cotton, coffee, sugar, rice, fruits and their main crops of watermelons and tobacco. Living around the lake and using it as their source of freshwater were, naturally enough, fishermen. Of typical Indian build they were short with copper coloured skin and straight dark hair though some of these 3,000 inhabitants had an obvious Spanish ancestry. These were the descendents of the

Chorotega tribe and were still using Aztec words in their language.

Travelling to the opposite end of the island near Madera, he found a different people: 'of commanding stature, many of the men being over six feet high, and the women proportionally large'. These people, he believed, were the remnant of an even older tribe, already inhabiting the islands when the Chorotega arrived.

'There are traditions pointing that way and these people are more reticent and suspicious than the others, seeming still to have reverence for their ancient gods, and showing no disposition to guide me to their idols.'

Bransford found many remains of the ancient peoples and with much local help he scientifically excavated and documented a number of pre-Colombian archaeological sites. Even then, he found one important site quite ransacked, the owner digging up and selling the spectacular artefacts to the brisk pre-Colombian trade with no effort to record and conserve. Large pottery urns, round and shoe shaped, many with raised designs of animals and figures in a minimalistic style were already known but it was Bransford who realised that besides their household uses, they were sometimes used as funary urns. After death the bodies were possibly kept until desiccated before burial, a practice that was still being used by tribes in Costa Rica at that time. The body was then placed, fully articulated, in a sitting position inside an urn, a cap put over the opening and then buried. Many of these urns were found around the beaches, sometimes so closely packed that they were touching. Buried with them was food, beans, seeds, coffee and corn; stone implements, shells and beads, both terra cotta and green argillite and jadeite and occasionally small gold creatures. Squier, visiting in 1849 dearly wanted one of these small gold statues as a memento after having seen a golden frog on Omotepe. Even though he said that he would buy one at any cost, none were forthcoming.

The green artefacts are very special as green is the sacred colour of the natives throughout the Americas, green stone ornaments found by the Spanish were held in the highest esteem, the god Quetzelcoatl having taught the art of working green stone. There is even a myth that there is an emerald mine deep in the waters of lake Cocibolca protected by the sharks and stories of bodies being sacrificed to the sharks in reverence.

Many of the urns had caps to match the pot, but others had what looked like up-turned bowls over them. These and similarly worked bowls were quite different from the workmanship of the urns and this style has been called luna ware, after the owner of the hacienda where it was first found. They are elaborately decorated with grotesque faces, sometimes in relief; snakes which have great symbolic significance and other animals. Stylish, zigzag, geometric designs in brown and red, on backgrounds of cream or beige, circle around the pots and sometimes rootlets had been burned into the design to create delicate irregular bluish lines. Bransford considered that this style of pottery was absolutely unique and:

'...could not be mistaken or confounded with other prehistoric American ware by the most careless observer'.

He also wondered whether:

'...different people had manufactured the two varieties and that to commerce or conquest was due the interchange of articles'.

Other pottery was found including a black polished style and the magnificent pieces that we easily recognise today as pre-Colombian, terra cotta bowls and tripods with sculpted feet shaped like birds or animals or monsters, bowls with grotesque faces protruding and all lavishly decorated, some with the characteristic plumed serpent of the Aztecs. It was amongst these finds that Bransford found the skeletons with painted bowls carefully placed over the skull before burial. There were decorated axes, whistles and terracotta figures of men, women and children.

In addition to all this pottery Bransford was shown rocks with stone carvings of spirals, figures, faces and pictographs, many in caves at the waters edge and even underwater, only appearing at low lake levels. Most spectacular of all, though already known, were the large five foot high basalt stone images, usually found in pairs, a man and a woman carved:

'...with a grim simplicity and massiveness in their appearance, very different from the elaborately and curiously ornamented idols of the Aztecs'.

The volcanic nature of the island had left these basalt rocks strewn over the ground and they had been transformed into statues of people:

'...a male sitting, with a sullen, cruel expression of face; the lips thick and everted. It had a headdress representing the head of some large animal'.

Another of a woman, possibly giving birth and a man:

'...sitting with his long arms hanging down by the sides of the seat. The fingers, toes, genitals and buttocks were well carved'.

The quantity of artifacts he found were extensive and Bransford suggested that some of the remains were 'of great antiquity', pre-dating the Chorotega Indian movement onto the island as they showed no aztec or mayan influence. Some sources have suggested that they may be as old as 4,000 years. He believed that the stone statues and rock carvings might be some of the earliest remains in the Americas. A tantalising glimpse of some ancient, almost unknown, civilization and the possibility that Nicaraguas pre-Colombian history may have begun on the lake islands.

There are other islands even more mysterious than Omotepe. When Squier travelled the country he was fascinated and amazed by much he saw, not least by the ancient stone statues. On Pensacola island one statue was nine feet tall and ten feet in circumference, a man with massive limbs and a broad prominent chest crouching, hands resting on his thighs. Above his head rose a monstrous head and jaws of some animal. The carving was forceful and free;

'...I have never seen a statue which conveyed so forcibly the idea of power and strength'.

Zapatera is ten kilometres by five and a half kilometres and is another volcanic, basalt rock island with a peak 600 metres high and covered with thick forest that hides a crater lake in the centre.   The island is rough and rocky with dangerous banks but many small bays.   Concealed amongst the plants are valuable archaeological remains of a religious site and a burial ground of a pre-Colombian culture and extraordinary rock carvings.   Here, Squier found more huge stone statues, 15 perfect or nearly perfect statues, some standing, others seated, some carved with symbolic symbols.

'A superstitious feeling...began to creep over me.   On one side steep cliffs, against which the waters of the lake chafed with a subdued roar, and upon the other was the deep, extinct crater, with its black sides and sulphurous lake; in truth a weird place, not unfittingly chosen by the aboriginal priesthood as the theatre of their strange and gloomy rites.'

Squier lay back on the stone where he had been sitting.

'My limbs fell into place as if the stone had been made to receive them – my head was thrown back, and my breast raised; a second, and the thought crossed my mind with startling force 'the stone of sacrifice'.   I leaped up with a feeling half of alarm.   I observed the stone more closely: it was a rude block altered by art, and had beyond question been used as a stone of sacrifice.'

Most of the statues he found were carved from a single block of basalt, some with a monster or animal head above or surrounding the human head but which left the face showing clearly, though one had a mask through which the tongue protruded.   Squier suspected that this statue had a profound symbolic significance.   There was a tiger (a jaguar) in a sitting position with its paws resting upon its belly.

'I easily comprehended the awe with which it probably was regarded by the people, in whose religious system it entered as the significant emblem of power mightier than that of man.'

Sadly, these artefacts are today in museums and private collections. To have seen them in their right place amongst the rocks and vegetation was, clearly, awe-inspiring.

During his visit to Zapatera he was told stories of a 14 inch by 8 inch animal statue 'couchant' carefully preserved by the Indians at the summit of a high secluded point on the island where:

'...they secretly retreated to pour out libations before it and perform rites; the nature of which none would reveal'.

It took more than 50 years to find this particular place, and the statue, which is now in the Smithsonian Museum.

Zapatera is surrounded by an arc of isletas and, on one of these, the Isla de Muerte, can be seen very curious, very ancient inscriptions. One more glimpse into the past.

Not so far away, deep in the jungles north of the Rio San Juan, rumours of stone structures have been around for at least a hundred years and, if they were true would suggest that the river had been used by people for very much longer than was originally thought. In February 2006, in a newspaper article it was revealed that during the Sandanista/Contra war, over 20 years ago, a reconnaissance plane over-flew the region behind the San Juan and what they thought they had found was extraordinary. Pyramids, albeit of rough design were seen in the overgrown jungle, that they believed was a pre-Colombian, Nahualt civilization complex, complete with mausoleum. The article said that the find had been kept quite secret, the military guarding the site. However, other archaeological sources say that although rough pyramids have been found in the north of the country, there are no pyramids near the San Juan or any buildings, just a suggestive collection of basalt rocks. And, people say, if it did exist, how could anyone keep something like that secret for 20 years in Nicaragua!

When Walker first saw Omotepe he described it as:

'...rising as Venus from the sea the tall and graceful cone of Omotepe. The dark forests of the tropics clothed the sides of the volcano...The beholder would not have been surprised to see it wake at any time.'

Omotepe had been the exclusive possession of the Indians, no white man could live there without their permission and an American/German family who wanted to start a cotton plantation were murdered around 1845. Even in 1860 it was difficult to find anyone who would take a foreigner to the island but Walker ignored this and turned it into a hospital.

It was to this paradise that the sick and injured came in 1856. The first of the evacuees sent from Granada were in a seriously bad way. These were the ill and injured. Just travelling the kilometre from Granada to the pier had been traumatic. They had staggered and limped, tried to support each other, used rifles and anything else that came to hand as crutches. Those that were completely unable to walk were pushed in hand carts over the cobbled streets, jolting and jarring all the way. They were taken on board one of the steamships to Omotepe by way of La Virgen where more ill and injured were taken on board. The situation on the ship was ghastly, there were the ill, whilst others had untreated sores and injuries of all kinds. There was no treatment and bandages were covered with blood, puss and flies whilst rats ran free. The stench was so bad that it had the crew scrambling for the top decks and fresh air.

By the time they reached Omotepe, many had died in the cold, damp night and the survivors now had to get ashore. This was no easy task, and possibly the worst part of the whole experience as they had to be lowered eight feet, down to a barge, for the trip to shore. Many were screaming and moaning from injuries whilst others just stoically endured. Once on land they were carried to the village but 24 had to be left on the beach that first night. At the end of all this misery they found an amazing group of people, and comfort. This group comprised the mix of Captain John M. Baldwin, whom had been left on the island accidentally and a rancher, Charles Myers. In addition there was the mayor, his wife and two other women; the only people left in the village after it was abandoned once it had become known that it was to be used as an hospital as, understandably, the villagers had fled from fear of disease.

The women set to, and provided a cooked meal for everyone in the village, and soup for those on the beach. This act certainly kept some alive that would otherwise have died but, even so, some did not survive that night. Another group of 60 soldiers, women and children that arrived later did not help the situation, nor some, albeit half-hearted attack and looting by annoyed Indians. When Walker learnt what was happening, he moved everyone to San Jorge and went there himself, together with the remnants of his filibusters; but events were occurring about which he knew nothing.

Chapter 17   River Battles

Vanderbilt wanted the transit company back, and he had money. Together with Mora in Costa Rica, who hoped to get a share of any profits, he put into effect a plan to re-take the river and he, as well as the British, supplied the Costa Ricans with arms and money. They decided to approach the San Juan via the Rio San Carlos. Under the command of sergeant major Maximo Blanco they left in December, the height of the rainy season. The boats they were expecting on the San Carlos had not materialised so they built rafts. When in the water these fell apart, hit tree trunks and other debris flowing down the river; they overturned and armaments, guns, cannon and ammunition were lost. The men were wet, disgruntled, hungry and argumentative. Their plans changed and instead of heading for Greytown, they decided to take the small filibuster defense at La Trinidad. Hiding against the bank on their rafts, too scared to move in case they capsized, they spent the night near the outpost. The next morning some 130 of these men approached through the jungle and found the filibusters eating breakfast. Some 45 minutes later, it is thought that only six of the 60 filibusters present survived the attack whilst the breakfast was being devoured by the Costa Ricans.

From La Trinidad, using seconded boats they headed for Greytown on a dark, grey, glowering day; it was pouring with rain and a storm had whipped up waves that were threatening to swamp the boats. Wet and cold they approached the mouth of the San Juan around 2.00 am and headed for Greytown and Punta Arenas. Before daylight they had captured four steamboats and the transit buildings. Everybody came out to watch the proceedings, as it seemed more like an entertainment than an invasion. The Costa Ricans were in charge and there was very little that anybody could do about it. The Costa Rican flag was raised and the four steamers, the Wheeler, the Machuca, the Morgan and the Bulwer left that day, Christmas Eve, for San Carlos, their crews quite happy to accept the terms of the new owners.

The Wheeler and the Machuca were left below the Sarapiqui whilst the other two, the Morgan and the Bulwer, went on to La Trinidad where they picked up 70 soldiers that had travelled there overland. The Bulwer was sent to pick up 800 men under the command of General Mora, brother of the Costa Rican president, who had been cutting their way through jungle trails with machetes to a rendezvous on the San Juan, which amazingly, they made. Blanco, in the Morgan, headed upstream to El Castillo, where, masquerading as filibusters, they took the town. Then, by pretending that they were passengers wanting passage on the river, they took the Ogden. At this point Walker's men in El Castillo fort, fled.

The Ogden continued upstream to find La Virgen near the rapids. This, the second largest steamship, was a prize and she was quickly boarded and overcome. She turned out to be an even better prize than they thought as, along with the cannon, rifles and ammunition, she had a huge amount of provisions and alcohol on board. Blanco and his men set up camp on the riverbank and they drank and ate whilst waiting for the Bulwer to arrive with Mora and his men. After three days, when the Bulwer still hadn't arrived and after much feasting, Blanco ordered his men to San Carlos. The La Virgen was made ready and she puffed upstream. Just before reaching San Carlos 40 men left the ship for the shore, to approach San Carlos on foot.

The fort at San Carlos had had no word of what was happening on the river and when La Virgen gave her normal signal, the filibuster commander of the fort went out to the ship for the normal inspection and was promptly taken prisoner. Blanco lied, and told him that there were 500 men on shore and ready to attack the fort. At this news the commander decided that surrender was the better part of valour. With the capture of San Carlos on January 1st 1857, the whole of the San Juan was now in Costa Rican hands. For Walker the cost had been heavy, 4,000 American lives had been lost by now, including two of his brothers. Only 400 of his men remained.

Walker always maintained that it was more important to control the lake rather than the river but, without control of the river, all transport along the waterway was at the mercy of whoever did hold the river Walker was unaware that the river had been taken and neither did the San Carlos, the largest of the steamboats which was packed with passengers, perhaps as many as 400, and was heading across the lake to San Carlos and the river. On arrival at San Carlos the true situation was quickly discovered and, making the passengers the priority, the ship surrendered to the Costa Ricans who now controlled almost all the waterway. They allowed the San Carlos, with its passengers, to go on to El Castillo where they were all transferred to another steamer for the trip to Greytown.

Plans to oust Walker were progressing slowly, General Mora was enjoying his control of the waterway, travelling along the river and across the lake even to Granada, but he dared not set foot on land there as Henningsen had set fire to it less than a month earlier, it was rife with cholera and there was still a stench of rotting bodies. What Mora was not doing, was tending to business. Supplies were not getting through from Costa Rica and the men at El Castillo and La Trinidad did not have enough food and many were ill. Walker was with Henningsen at Rivas on the land route section and preparing for an attack and he was well stocked, his supplies arriving via San Juan del Sur on the Pacific. San Jorge had been taken but Henningsen was sent with 400 men to recover it. On arrival they found the streets barricaded and Walker was later to remark.

'...the rapidity with which Central American troops throw up barricades is almost incredible and they are more expert at such work than even a Paris mob'.

San Jorge proved tenacious and as Henningsen still had troops that were overindulging in the local alcohol, he withdrew after 40 were killed. Walker was still confident that recruits would soon be arriving from the United States and he dearly needed them as he was reduced to around 500 men from 1,000, though the allied forces of Nicaraguans and Costa Ricans were down to 2,000 men from 7,000. A ship did appear with 20 men but Mora had news of it and by offering food, protection and free passports they, and others of Walker's men, deserted him. Notwithstanding, Walker went ahead and with Henningsen attacked again with a total complement of 400 men and seven guns. The town was prepared, they were expected and the fight lasted many hours. Walker was hit in the throat by a spent ball, for the second time, and they again retreated, defeated. Meanwhile, Rivas had been attacked but the local troops held it for Walker. At the other end of the river Greytown was still in filibuster hands, and they were getting recruits.

General Mora received news of this and immediately dispatched troops to strengthen the river base at La Trinidad. Eventually, some 300 men were encamped there. It was the height of the rainy season and La Trinidad was a swamp; also, someone had neglected to send any food. It was pouring with rain, the troops were hungry, had inadequate protection and were waiting to be attacked by man and beast.

The Sarapiqui was overflowing and there was dysentery. Many deserted on the first day.

Meanwhile at Greytown, the filibusters were completely stranded across the estuary at Punta Arenas due to Vanderbilt's conniving, and by Britain who kept the guns of a British naval ship trained on their camp. They planned their attack and refuelled an old steamboat, The Rescue, and left for La Trinidad. There was a short engagement that ended with The Rescue retreating, which gave the Cost Rican and allied troops time to reorganise. The filibusters then set up a second position, directly across the river to La Trinidad, and eventually, more than two weeks later, after being under heavy fire, the sick and wounded at La Trinidad were ordered to leave. The cannons were heaved to the bottom of the river and the remaining men retreated to San Jose in Costa Rica. The filibusters took over the fort, threw the dead into the river in the hope that the bodies would escape the sharks, drift downstream and out to sea and demoralize the British.

El Castillo was next. A British soldier of fortune, Captain Caulty, was fighting with the allies and received news that the filibusters were on their way. There were few defences to counter an attack on the town but he tried to save the ships. Two he was able to send upstream but the other two steamships that were moored in the town he ordered be burnt, rather than let them be captured. On arrival, the filibusters, even though under fire, were able to save The Scott but The Machuca was lost. They tried to negotiate a surrender of the fort but the filibuster commander, Titus, was a fool. Caulty was stalling but managed to get Titus to agree to a 24 hour truce and he immediately reinforced the fort with troops from San Carlos. The Morgan appeared with 77

Rio San Juan

armed men and the filibusters barely escaped with their lives, retreating in the Scott.

Whilst this action was going on at El Castillo, a boat with 135 Texas Rangers for Walker came charging up the river from Greytown for a new attack on Castillo but after meeting and talking with the retreating troops in the Scott, they decided that it was too dangerous to go barrelling on upstream and so returned to Greytown to join Walker via Panama. However, they stopped at La Trinidad to assess the situation there and a number of the rangers, officers and men transferred to the Scott. Then there was a most horrendous accident. A member of the crew tried to cool an overheating cylinder by throwing river water over it. The explosion was catastrophic. The ship was destroyed, 20 died immediately, 40 were injured with dreadful scalds and burns and broken and missing limbs. Many died later of the horrific injuries, survivors begging to be killed and put out of their misery, one witness describing them as 'living meat'. When The Rescue arrived she lived up to her name and took the mangled survivors to Greytown. Some to beg the British warship in the harbour to, please, just take them back to the United States.

Walker meanwhile was, again, having problems. The allies, albeit with squabbling commanders, were closing in on him from both the lake and from San Juan del Sur where the United States warship The Mary was at anchor. Henningsen was asked to attend a conference with its captain, Captain Davis, on the ship. There Henningsen was urged to tell Walker to surrender and that he would be given safe passage. Walker realising that his situation was hopeless, surrendered to Davis, along with his men, and the ship sailed from Nicaragua on May 1st 1857 for the United States. There he was greeted as a hero but once the press discovered that his men were sick or injured, lice ridden, half starved and dressed in rags, he was vilified.

This, though, was not quite the last of Walker. He and his filibusters had left Nicaragua and the foreign troops that had helped in his ejection had left too: but not the Costa Ricans. They kept control of the river, the steamers, Greytown, La Trinidad and El Castillo whilst the politicians were still arguing. Costa Rica claimed the river and declared that she had the right to use the lake. They even tendered for bids for a new transit route company and even gave a 99 year contract to a French man, but after he was nearly killed in a steamship accident, little more was heard from him. Internal Nicaraguan political differences were abandoned and preparations for war against Costa Rica were made. An attempt at a negotiated settlement was being made when news came that Walker was back

Walker always believed that he would have won had the United States not interfered so he returned to Nicaragua with 200 men and a substantial amount of supplies. He steamed into Punta Arenas where, mistaken for a company transit ship, he anchored. A horrified United States warship commander watched as Walker and his men calmly disembarked and made camp knowing that they could not be arrested as they were on foreign soil.

Prior to landing at Punta Arenas, Walker had sent 50 troops in three boats up the Colorado with orders to prepare the way for an attack. La Trinidad they found deserted, El Castillo was abandoned on their approach, the Ogden and the Morgan at anchor. Further upriver they captured the Vanderbilt at the El Toro rapids.

Nicaraguan troops had been sent after Walker as soon as he had made his appearance at Punta Arenas and it was there that he was arrested. A message was sent upriver to his dismayed troops at El Castillo who, in retaliation, disabled the Vanderbilt, spiked the cannon and plundered the fort before returning to Punta Arenas.

On December 15th 1857 Walker and his men left Nicaragua again, this time never to return. This was also the end of the first United States involvement in Nicaraguan politics.

Nicaragua was completely devastated and demoralised, Granada was burnt and feared another attack by Walker. With little discussion or argument, Nicaragua signed a treaty that recognised Costa Rica's annexation of the Guanacaste and the right of Costa Rican boats to navigate freely on part of the San Juan, as long as they were only engaged in transporting commercial goods.

Walker went to Honduras where he was again calling for volunteers to start another revolution but a British ship demanded his surrender or his departure. He chose the latter and marched out of Truxillo with 28 men but was forced to fight when he was surprised by a group of Honduran troops at Cotton Tree where he suffered facial injuries. By December 25th he had reached the Rio Negro, two and a half miles from the Atlantic, where he felt himself safe and where he rested for three days. Here the British, found him and demanded to see him. Walker was still declaring that he was the President of Nicaragua and refusing to give up his sword until he knew it was to an officer;

'Yes, you surrender to me as a British Officer.'

He was handed over to the Hondurans, tried and shot on the 12 September 1860. Had he declared his nationality as American, he would have escaped the death penalty. He was 30 years old.

Chapter 18 Greytown and The Bar

Arriving at the mouth of the San Juan is something of an anticlimax. Forget all thoughts of a beautiful forested estuary widening out into the clear turquoise waters of the Caribbean with golden beaches and colourful fish swimming around heads of coral. The reality is a huge sand bar that crosses the whole of the estuary, except for a small gap that can be negotiated only with difficulty and only at high tide by anything larger than a canoe. It was this sand bar that fooled the early explorers and was probably the reason why it took so long to find the mouth of the San Juan.

We pulled the canoe up onto the bar and walked up a sand slope to the top of the sand ridge, and there was the Atlantic, looking just like the North Sea, grey and rough with waves breaking sideways onto a black sand beach in a froth of bubbles. This was not a spot to take out your towel, sunscreen, sunshade and a good book. The gritty, black sand of the bar has rubbish stranded along it and sometimes packets of drugs. When customs vessels get too close to boats trafficking the drugs from the Colombian owned islands off the North coast of Nicaragua they are thrown overboard, and end up on the beaches. Fishermen gut their catches here and the entrails are surrounded by coal black vultures pecking and fighting over the scraps. There is a turtle shell picked clean by birds, ants and crabs; and a pile of turtle eggshells alongside; an alarming sight.

Thomas Belt, the gold miner and naturalist, arrived on the 16th February, 1868 to superintend some gold mines in Nicaragua. Had he arrived twenty years earlier there would have been an excellent harbour with a U shaped entrance but, as more water veered off into the Rio Colorado, the harbour silted up so that ships, including Belt's, had to anchor outside and:

Rio San Juan

'...the shallow but dangerous bar has to be crossed'.

All that he could see from his ship:

'...was the sandy beach on which the white surf was breaking, a fringe of bushes with a few coconut palms holding up their feathery crowns, and in the distance a low background of dark foliage'.

Crossing the bar was dangerous. The treacherous currents and riptides had caused many shipwrecks and:

'...what adds to the horror and perhaps has unnerved many a man at a critical moment, is that large sharks swarm about the entrance to the river. We saw the fin of one rising above the surface of the water.'

The outlet of the San Juan may count as one of the most dangerous in the world for shark attack; the bull shark, *Carcharhinus leucas*, is common and considered a very aggressive animal. It breeds in the salty water outside the bar but can travel freely between salt and fresh water. Still common off the bar, in the sea and the lagoons, they are now only occasionally found in the river and the lake. Bull sharks have a ferocious reputation that is well earned as they will feed on just about anything and are probably responsible for more deaths than the great white shark. . The bull shark can sense a drop of blood at 100 metres and, of ships that capsized in the lake or river few people lived to tell the tale. The victims of the last major shark attack in the lake were those from a light plane crash in the 1960s leaving no survivors. In 1872 a US surveying expedition lost six men when trying to cross the bar in heavy weather:

'…only a few mangled remnants were ever found'.

More recently, a boat with 28 passengers from Bluefields sank and only twelve survived. Many people have been taken by sharks, crocodiles and alligators in the estuary and the San Juan and Indio rivers, swimming an activity only undertaken in quiet backwaters and today, when the shark numbers are rising, it can be a nervous exercise.

Belt had an easy trip of it.

'Getting into one of the canoes with my boxes, I was rapidly paddled towards the shore. When we reached the bar we were dexterously taken over it – the Caribs waited just outside until a higher wave than usual came rolling in, then paddling with all their might we were carried over on its crest, and found ourselves in the smooth water of the river.'

We strolled along the bar with a few seagulls and a mangy dog for company and could find absolutely nothing of the transit company base at Punta Arenas. No signs of alligators either. Belt on a later trip to Greytown was staying with the British Consul who had been out on the bar shooting alligators as he wanted a skull. Belt was walking along the bar and had passed the dead one that the Consul had shot, and many others over 15 feet in length.

'One lay motionless and thinking it was another dead one, I was walking up to it, and had got within three yards when I saw the film over its eye moving….. I went back a short distance to look for a stick to throw at it: but when I turned again the creature was just disappearing into the water. …I had the feeling that I had escaped a great danger.'

Once over the bar, Belt discovered a harbour that was silting up:

'Weedy banks filled the once spacious harbour and cattle waded amongst the long grass, where, within the last twenty years a frigate has lain at anchor. Wading and aquatic birds were abundant in the marshes, white cranes and chocolate-brown jacana. A large alligator lazily crawled off a mud-spit into the water, where he floated, showing only his back above the surface.'

It was with relief that we got into our canoe and away from the bar to explore the beautiful lagoons behind, the Bahia de San Juan. Very little seemed to have changed from Belt's day.

'…the land is quite level, and interspersed with lakes and ponds with much marshy ground.'

There were waterlilies and reeds and fish jumping, the same birds, but the manatees Belt saw are now rare. The green parrots still:

'… fly over in screaming flocks, or nestle in loving couples amidst the foliage'

whilst toucans:

'...hop along the branches, turning their long, highly-coloured beaks from side to side with an old-fashioned look'.

One of the luxury hotels in Nicaragua is here on a lagoon and a couple of days later, we were longing for its comfort. We rounded a bend and there was a huge metal structure rusting away in the middle of the lagoon, a habitat for the ferns and epiphytes that covered it whilst the iron struts were perches for birds. Not the frigate, it was one of the enormous dredges from the 1890s, left over from a failed attempt to build a trans-isthmus canal. We gazed at it, then headed off for New Greytown,

Greytown, in the 1800s was sited on the bank of the lagoon and had a population of 500, many of whom were foreigners. There were two main streets more than half a kilometre in length and running parallel to the shore and lined by houses. There were American style buildings including a two-storey hotel, government buildings and American, French and British consulates. There were bars and gaming houses, brothels and shops

In May of 1849, sailing in a brig from the United States laden with freight that included pigs, poultry, water casks, tar barrels, spars and tarpaulins was the 28 year old Ephraim George Squier, the first ministerial level diplomat to be sent from the United States to Central America. He landed in Greytown 26 days later and some 20 years before Belt. He described a street of:

'...huts make of boards but most of reeds and all thatched with palm, canoes drawn up to them and a boiler from a steamer abandoned on the shore. In the centre an open space and a larger building with a flagstaff and a dingy flag resembling the Union Jack, this the customs house and the flag that of the 'King of the Mosquitoes' the ally of Great Britain and what the British facetiously call the 'Mosquito Kingdom'.'

There was no school, no church and the priest, most likely to be found:

'...at the residence of the prettiest of the nut-brown senoritas'.

The region has been inhabited for a long time and the intermingling of peoples is quite apparent in the population of Greytown. In Squier's day the population of about 300 included the English authorities, Negroes from Jamaica and a multi-hued blend of white, Indian, Negro, mestizo – black, brown, yellow and fair. This cultural mix nearly reflected that of Nicaragua as a whole, Squier later putting that at 18,000 blacks, 30,000 Europeans, 96,000 Indians and 156,000 mixed. The women:

'...wore their clothes loose and their hair braided into two long locks like schoolgirls. They puffed cigars and a few walked through the mud in grubby silk or satin shoes. Doors were open to catch the air, hammocks swinging. Behind the town was dense tropical forest, nothing but dense dark solitudes where the tapir and the wild boar roamed unmolested; where the painted macaw and the noisy parrot, flying from one great ceiba to another, alone disturbed the silence; and where the many hued and numerous serpents of the tropics coiled among the branches of strange trees loaded with flowers and fragrant with precious gums.'

And of the lagoon he commented on the beautiful women washing clothes in the water and on seeing two or three huge alligators a companion called them:

'devils in an earthly paradise'.

Local children muttered that there were:

'…many snakes here',

Borne out by the fact that two men had been bitten and died a few days earlier.

Squier had been taken to a house where he could stay but was not amused when, after his four-day stay he was presented with a bill for $8, about double the going rate, particularly as he had made a list of the wildlife that could be found in the house, that included scorpions, lizards, house snakes and cockroaches.

Mark Twain arrived in 1866 and wrote of brisk businesses selling goods and services to the transients, and:

'…some nice vacant lots'.

In 1868 Belt described Greytown as:

'…neat white-painted houses, with plume-crowned palms rising amongst and over them. Greytown, though only a small place is one of the neatest tropical towns that I have visited. The houses are well built of wood. Pretty gardens surround or front many of them, others are nearly hidden amongst palms and breadfruit, orange, mango and other tropical fruit trees. The squares, the open spaces and many of the streets are covered with short grass that makes a beautiful sward to walk on.'

And the British consulate as:

'….one of the most attractive sights in Greytown'.

Another early traveller a Mr. Baldwin, also had good things to say about Greytown:

'The steep thatch-roofed cane houses clustered together at its (the bay's) head relieving the dense forest behind; and the dimly seen summits of the far-off mountains of Nicaragua made to me one of the most beautiful landscapes that I have ever beheld.'

But another visitor had a quite different perspective:

'…a more disgusting place I never saw….swarming with reptiles and repulsive roots and darnels, rank and rotting.'

And the minimal dress of the locals was a cause for concern by some:

'…girls with patches of flesh showing here and there'.

Trade was vigorous; coffee, indigo, hides, cacao, sugar, tobacco, wood and rubber being exported to the US and England and Greytown was thriving as it was considered a healthier place to live than others similar towns, only a few feet above water, flat, with mangroves and water all around. Squier talked about the apparent healthiness of the town:

> '...whereas, only half a mile away, on the opposite bank with a greater depth of water immediately fronting it, it is fatal to those who may attempt to occupy it'.

A settlement was built on this bank but within two months it was abandoned, everybody there moving back to the other bank. Belt was a geologist by training and thought that this 'healthiness' may be to do with the situation of the town, with no hills behind allowing the steady trade winds to:

> '...carry off emanations from the soil'.

Possibly the winds made life for the mosquitoes more difficult but they took their toll on human life in Greytown as elsewhere. Belt also thought that the porous soil might have had something to do with it and other writers described a pure drinking water system where water was filtered into barrels placed in the soil. This clean drinking water could be the sole reason for the relative healthiness of the population.

Today, all that remains are the cemeteries, Catholic, American, Masonic and Anglican. The pleasing town with steamships lining the banks and travelling up and down the river, a vision of the past.

Rio San Juan

Chapter 19   New Greytown

New Greytown is sited on the Rio Indio, a straight, wide river, that flows parallel to the coast but then disappears in a maze of tributaries. The town was rebuilt after the Sandanista/Contra war in 1990 on it's new site with concrete block pathways and wooden houses, raised above the soggy ground. The Caribbean lowlands of Nicaragua are the wettest areas in Central America, hot and rainy much of the year, partly due to those healthy north east trade winds and a spectacular rainfall of as much as 6,500 millimetres in a year.

We docked the canoe and checked in at the customs house and MARENA office and looked for somewhere to stay. We should have paid the $350 dollars for a night at the hotel on the lagoon and luxuriated with a massage, cold beer and an excellent meal, instead of the best the town had to offer, a dirty bedroom and bathroom, no hot water, and lumpy, questionable pillows. When we arrived there was no water or electricity as the town generator only worked between 4.00pm and 11.00pm and we were too early. A cold shower was eventually available, bliss to get clean and cold water not as bad as it sounds. Many Nicaraguans will ask "why do foreigners want hot water when the weather is so hot?".

We found a bar with a cold Victoria beer, rice and prawns but with deafening music even when, grudgingly, it was turned down. A young man joined us who worked as a nature guide at the big lodge and who told us that nearly everyone it employed was from the town. The fishing was good, he said, both in the river and out in the ocean, that most of the clients were from the United States and Costa Rica and came to fish but there were forest trails and boats and canoes for river trips. It all sounded pretty nice, if expensive. Not wanting to indulge in noisy rounds of beer, rum and poker, to while away the night, and with all thoughts of reading a book gone with the impossibly low voltage lightbulbs and, as the mosquitoes were beginning to bite, all we could do was head back to our room and a very early night.

Next morning we bought some picnic food and set off down the Rio Indio which is separated from the sea by a fertile strip of land that is primarily used for farming, mainly fruits, and grazing and an old coconut plantation that was commandeered by the Sandanistas and where, in earlier times, Indians had collected turtles, manatee and alligators. Trees are not meant to be felled on this land as they form a buffer for New Greytown from the wind that sometimes blows off the sea, particularly important should there be a hurricane. Along the banks were wide stretches of reeds and, occasionally, a pole sticking up with a bucket on it, or maybe a cow skull, or just some fluttering fabric. These were door signs, entrances through the reeds, to houses built on solid ground inland. We glimpsed wooden houses, just about hanging together, with scavenging chickens and pigs and smoke from cooking fires rising vertical in the lifeless air.

We continued for a couple of hours still amazed by the river with its the now familiar plants, birds, and butterflies with huge blue Morphos electric against the green jungle. This river was a bit like driving down a new motorway in a heat haze, for one strange moment I thought I saw buildings in the distance, a lot of blocky shapes but they turned out to be clouds and their reflections, probably something to do with lack of sleep.

We were heading for yet another MARENA office where, we had been told the night before, we could get permission to go into the forest and walk a way along a trail. We moored at the office and one of the rangers came out to meet us. Although they are paid next to nothing, they are supplied with a very attractive safari style uniform and always look smart and clean. We produced our passports and Joe his residency and anything else we could think of that we might have with us. But, where was our permit? We did not have a permit. Nobody had said anything about a permit, not even when we had asked at the police station in New Greytown. No amount of charm could persuade him to let us go any further.

We turned back and headed for one of the really pretty tributaries that we had passed on the way. We were now on a country road rather than a superhighway, the water headed deep into the forest, the trees reached over us and we had to duck under the lowest branches. White spider lilies grew along the bank and yellow water lilies lay in the water before them, dragonflies perched on their leaves. A weather front had followed us and the dull sky made the forest look flat, like a stage-set, the only sounds those of fish jumping and birds singing. We turned into another, even smaller, tributary and pulled onto the bank for lunch at what was obviously a well-used landing place. On a closer inspection there were chips of wood and long poles used for manipulating trunks. It seemed that trees were being cut and the wood worked for new canoes and the repair of old ones. The indigenous Indians have lived with the forest, as have their forefathers for, possibly, hundreds of years and getting them on the side of conservation is not easy.

Joe had decided that he wanted a boat, a wooden canoe, so the search was on. At one of the landing sites we came across an old man, Mauricio, and his grandson repairing a canoe, carving new braces for the inside. In our unfluent Spanish but with Joe's knack of always getting understood, we managed to describe what we wanted and he gave us a price for a wooden canoe. The boy, Marco, never raised his head from the piece of wood he was carving until, with a shy glance, he waved us goodbye. We left them some bread, cheese, fruit and granola bars and went on our way.

We were entranced by the beauty of the forest, vines as delicate as thread and as thick as rope twisted and looped around the trees; plants climbed and cascaded with strident flowers. Epiphytes adorned branches and scattered through the trees were the white trunks and huge silver fingered leaves of the Cecropias whilst on the water the exquisite tiny, 1-2 centimetre, lace-like pink leaves of a fern floated on the surface between the lily pads. Called mosquito fern, it covers the water surface and chokes out mosquito larva and is often used as a pond ornamental to control mosquitoes and also by rice farmers in Asia as it has nitrogen-fixing bacteria in its leaves and is a natural fertilizer.

Large, long woven nests of the oropendulas hung over the water. The trapeze artists of the bird world they turn complete somersaults around tree branches during their nodding, bowing displays all the while making bottle-emptying gurgles. Life and survival in the colony is not always easy as toucans, snakes, small mammals and bats feed on the eggs and for the young the main problem is the botfly larva. The eggs are laid by the fly directly on the chicks and once they hatch the chick cannot survive. Some oropendulas build their nests close to wasp nests, as the wasp will attack the botfly; but there is another alliance. The cowbird, which is related to the oropendula, is a parasite, like the cuckoo, and when it has an opportunity, it lays its eggs in an oropendula nest where they are hatched and the young cared for by the oropendula foster mother. The young oropendulas do very well from this association as the cowbird chicks preen the other birds in the nest and pick off the botfly eggs and larva. However, this only happens in colonies that are not near wasp nests as there, the oropendulas chase away the cowbirds; the two arrangements seem not to co-exist.

There were large round cannon-ball like fruit hanging from branches over the river and whilst looking at these we caught the eye of a green and brown iguana in the tree. Good to eat they are caught by the Indians and used to be very common, this was the biggest of the few that we saw.

A canoe paddled passed us, completely laden to within an inch of its waterline with platanos, it was going to New Greytown to catch the ferry to San Carlos tomorrow. What for us would be a trip of three hours would take him all day. We passed two men and a boy fishing by the bank and heard howler monkeys nearby, the telltale rustle in the treetops gave their position away and we watched them until they disappeared. We knew that the forest was crawling with wildlife but finding it is not easy, there was no access and no paths that you would dare to take on your own as the chance of getting lost and never finding a way out, even when only a few metres away from the river, was very real.

This tributary was busy. Another boat passed, this one laden with coconuts, two men, a boy, and a woman, all paddling. We had a boat jam as yet another canoe appeared going in the opposite direction. Everyone stopped and chatted and asked us where we were from. We all untangled ourselves and each went our own way. Where are they all going and coming from? Our map showed only a dead end and we wanted to go further and explore but we were some hours away from New Greytown and needed to be back before dark.

Back in town we complained to our friend, Melvin, a large friendly Afro-Caribbean/Indian mix gentleman about not being allowed down the river by the MARENA office.

"Oh, that's right, you have to get a permit from the MARENA office next door to the police station here before you go, I forgot that!"

Joe mentions that he really would like to have a wooden boat so off they go to the local boat builders. They see a really big boat that is being built, supposedly to ply between New Greytown and Bluefields on the Caribbean, another large canoe being repaired and a couple of others being fibre-glassed against the marine worms that will destroy a boat in a year if you are not careful. More prices quoted in dollars and colones and cordobas, and more measurements in varas, (33 inches) and yards, and meters. Area can be equally bemusing as it and can be described in hectares, square meters, acres and manzanas (1.74 acres). Conversations concerning measurements can be exotically confusing!

When Joe and Melvin got back we sat and talked and Melvin told us that they almost think of themselves as Costa Ricans. The only telephone system is a cell phone via Costa Rica, they use colones instead of cordobas as many of them work in nearby Tortuguero, one of Costa Rica's main tourist destinations. The electricity service in New Greytown is less than adequate and they are convinced that Costa Rica will supply them with better, (maybe) and cheaper, (unlikely) electricity.

The relationship between Costa Rica and Nicaragua has been turbulent. Costa Rica still has designs on the river and taken its grievance to the International Court. Nicaragua has never really forgiven Costa Rica for annexing the Guanacaste and the Nicoya Peninsula (rather attractive real estate nowadays) and 25 years later, during the William

Walker caper, for trying to take over the river, the lake and the trade route.

Today, Costa Rica has rights to the south shore of the river east of El Castillo and has limited rights of travel along the river but is demanding free access, as a right, to the entire river and to the Indo-Maiz reserve for their tourists. The peace-loving, environmentally friendly Costa Ricans are perceived in the world as the good guys, standing up to the war-like Nicaraguans fighting amongst themselves for a democracy, but driving their country into poverty and economic ruin whilst doing so. In fact many Costa Ricans had had many years of very lucrative jobs in Nicaragua under Somoza and gave assistance to the CIA funded Contra attacks. The human rights abuses in Costa Rica against Nicaraguan farm workers, in particular, are well documented and the claim of having no army does not get much credit either. The Costa Rican Civil Guard numbers are larger than the Nicaraguan army, and police force, combined and are well-trained combat troops.

In 1990 at the end of the Sandanista/Contra war, with Reagan gone and the Contras redundant, the winning Sandanistas organised elections that resulted in them being thrown out of power but they acknowledged the new government of Doña Violeta Barrios de Chamorro, leader of the anti-Sandanista grouping. Her task was immense, to change world attitude to Nicaragua. She put the army and police under civil control, reduced the numbers in the armed force, the Contras were disarmed but offered 1,600 square kilometres of land, much around the San Juan river. This, together with Sandanista land gifts has led to much blurring about who actually owns what, where.

In 1998 Costa Ricans in battle fatigues, and armed, were found patrolling the San Juan, which enraged the Nicaraguans. The battle of words has being going on ever since, Costa Rica being blamed for polluting the river by seepage from the enormous quantities of insecticides used in its banana plantations and being threatened with a ban on all shipping on the river. Costa Rica saying that if Nicaragua does not open up its natural resources to tourism, and money, then they will do it instead.

Recently more troops have been found on the river and at this moment Nicaragua waits for a legal decision, but a recent map from Costa Rica that shows them owning the San Juan has not been helpful and a Google earth map that also has the boundary wrong has only added to the tension.

Another night in our room in town after a game of dominoes and we consoled ourselves by listing the worst places where we had stayed, remote towns in Kenya and Ethiopia topped the list!

The ferry left at five in the morning so, at half past four, in the pitch dark we found our torches, dressed, tripped over each other in the small room but managed to pack our last few bits and pieces. We did know that the generator was not on in the mornings, unlike others we met who had packed nothing and had no handy torch. Even so, it was a bit chaotic. The evening before we had tied the canoe to the top of the ferry and stowed the engine, gas tanks and big box but there still seemed to be a lot of things. We felt our way along the path, with no light, as we had no spare hands to hold the torch, and made it to the ferry port with coffee on our minds. We reached the chain link fence but the entry door was firmly locked. There was nobody around. Ten minutes later, still nobody. It was now only five minutes before the ferry was due to leave.

"I bet they are on Costa Rican time." Joe finally came up with the answer.

Nicaragua decided to have a daylight savings exercise, though why, nobody was quite sure as nothing is really to be gained when you always have nearly 12 hours of daylight and 12 hours of night. We had already been caught out by it when taking my daughter to catch a flight to England and discovering that the airlines had not changed the times on their schedules. Now, it appeared, neither had the ferry. We had another hour to wait. Gradually people appeared and half an hour later the gates opened, and abruptly water was boiled, coffee made and cheese sandwiches on their way.

By six o'clock Costa Rican time, everything was loaded and off we went.

Chapter 20   Early River Travellers

In the middle of the 1800s the river was teeming with traffic, mainly canoes of all sizes but the bongo was king. Used by the Indians for hundreds of years and chosen by Calero and Machuca for their historic exploration, they were supreme. Hewn from single trunks of cedar, mahogany or ceiba, a lighter, softer wood that was less prone to split and was the wood of choice, the trees were shaped into canoes up to 45 feet long and six to seven feet wide, three feet deep and with a round prow and a square stern. The sides were raised by the addition of two extra planks of wood to give six feet of depth. They were strengthened with ribs, had a covered area to protect cargo at the rear and an awning set up for passengers. The oars were 15–16 feet long and poles were kept handy. Fully laden with sixteen tons of cargo, they drew only two to three feet of water but still got stuck on sandbars and had to be pushed off them, the crew balancing on boards attached across the front and back of the canoe for leverage. A bongo leaving the dock for the twenty to thirty day round trip to Granada was always an event and brought out a large audience, hawkers with drinks and snacks, fruits and cheese. A blast from a blown conch shell announced that the bongo was leaving, and it was off.

The bongo took six to nine days to get from Greytown to San Carlos, or 35-36 hours downstream. It had a crew of 8-22 oarsmen and a captain and as soon as it left port it would stop in midstream and, passengers or not, all the oarsmen would strip naked for the whole trip and then row for hours on end, perfectly synchronised. Thomas Belt recounts passing a bongo laden with cattle and indo-rubber.

'Poled by 12 bongo men, who have usually only one suit of clothes each, which they do not wear during the day, but keep stowed away under the cargo that it may be dry to put on at night. Their bronzed, glistening, naked bodies, as they ply their long poles together in unison, and chant some Spanish boat-song is one of the things that linger in the memory of the traveller up the San Juan.'

This tradition has, sadly, been abandoned.

The very real problem for the passengers was that there could be as many as 100 of them on board, which made it very crowded, particularly as they had to keep still to keep the boat steady so that the rowers could maintain their rhythm. It was a trip of extreme discomfort. In the words of one passenger:

'…couldn't move without turning the darn thing over and leaked badly besides.'

Passengers would stop at predestined places on the river, some of these exactly the same places where we had stayed on out trip down.

Collected by the gold mining company boat for the trip to San Carlos, Belt probably had it better than most and his description of the lower part of the river could have been written today. Staying close to shore to avoid the current:

'The banks at first were low and marshy and intersected by numerous channels, the principal tree was a long coarse-leaved palm, and there were great beds of wild cane and grass. As we proceeded up the river, the banks gradually became higher and drier, and we passed some small plantations of bananas and plantains made in clearings in the forest....The houses at the plantations were mostly miserable thatched huts with scarcely any furniture, the owners passing their time swinging in dirty hammocks, and occasionally taking down a canoe-load of plantains to Greytown for sale.'

At seven in the evening Belt had reached the branch of the Colorado river:

'The main body of water formerly flowed down past Greytown, and kept the harbour there open, but a few years ago, during a heavy flood, the river greatly enlarged and deepened the entrance to the Colorado Channel, and since then year by year the Greytown harbour has been silting up.'

His boat anchored in the mud for the night where he was plagued by mosquitoes and, as it poured with rain all night, this experienced international traveller deemed it:

'...one of the most uncomfortable nights I have ever passed.'

Four in the morning and they were on their way upriver:

'....the rain ceased, the mists cleared away, our spirits revived, and we forgot the discomforts of the night in admiration of the beauties of the river....a curtain of creeping and twining plants, many of which bore beautiful flowers, and the green was further varied here and there by the white stems of the Cecropia trees.'

On Squier's boat, his bongo men pulled into shore, built a fire and prepared a kettle with a layer of lard and then layers of plantain and beef sprinkled with salt until the pot was full, water added and the whole boiled until cooked. The night was spent moored in the river but Squier was protected from a light rain by an awning, though he did share it with a few mosquitoes. Before light they were on their way pausing only for a breakfast of broiled ham, fried plantain, bread and chocolate. Chocolate was a very important crop and cost effective as a single man could look after and harvest 1,000 trees.

At the Machuca rapids everything had to be portaged around them, passengers walked along the banks and all the cargo had to be carried, as for the boat itself, it could take some hours to navigate up the rapids. Squiers boat had no cargo and was, therefore, light; it was able to go straight up the rapids by keeping close to the right hand shore. It passed the wreck of the Orus and occasionally glanced off rocks but even so it still took 4 hours of strenuous work.

At El Diablo before El Castillo there was the same portage procedure but here the bongos would wait until another one or two arrived when the crews would take each boat up the rapids in turn, over the rocks and against the current, three to four time-consuming and exhausting hours for each boat to navigate this short stretch of the river. In the rainy season things could be even worse and sometimes departures had to be delayed as the rowers were unable to make any headway up the river. From El Castillo it was a relatively easy trip to San Carlos and the lake where, in Squier's boat, the crew all dived into the water, climbed back after a while and hunted for their clothes that had been put aside at Greytown.

'The economy, not to say the convenience, of going naked for the purpose of keeping ones clothes clean, was never more manifest. The whole crew dressed in clean attire which made us ashamed of our soiled garments.'

After a night in San Carlos they were off to Granada. When the NE trade winds were right, a sail would be raised to speed the boat the final stretch of the river and across the lake. On Squier's boat the bongo men set sail, leant back, lit cigars and played cards. Nothing could persuade them to row when there was any hint of a breeze. That evening was idyllic with;

'The sun sinking directly behind the peaks of Orosi (Omotepe) the islands of Solentiname and La Boqueta apparently floating in liquid 'gold',

But by midnight, after they had all fallen asleep in the calm waters, the lake was a raging tempest. The sail was frantically taken down, Ben, one of Squier's companions, eventually cutting the rope, and the crew rowed steadily and silently all night and into the bay of San Miguelito amongst the drinking cattle. Girls were taking jars to the lake for water and swimming like mermaids:

'…their long hair trailing like a veil'

and joshing with the crew:

"…how are you my darkeys?"

The next night they had reached Morito and here, after shooting at an alligator and after supper, three horsemen appeared with netting sacks containing four large square cheeses of 50lbs each of which were carefully placed on the bottom of the boat. Next day they continued on, past Omotepe and Zapatera, to Granada where they were met with a "goode by" or "California" by the children and girls whilst walking into town. Californians had already made a strong impression!

Other travellers were going the opposite way, down the river.

In October 1850 a group of people were making their way back to New York from San Francisco and elected to go via Nicaragua. They landed at Realejo in the north then went by cart to León, complaining about the $6.00 cost but noting that:

'The country is beautiful but a perfect wilderness....inhabited by Monkeys, Birds, and Serpents and beasts of prey'.

From León, which impressed them, they took the rough road to Granada where they provisioned for the six day voyage around the shoreline of Lake Cocibolca. They camped at night and during the day enduring heavy rain or blistering sun. San Carlos they found dingy and uninviting, its inhabitants:

'...most wretchedly poor'.

December 4th they left for San Juan de Nicaragua, which they reached two days later.

Another group, which included a diary writer a A.J.M. Letts took the same route, and commented that the natives were not against a little enterprise to extract money from the 'rich Californians' and described the following incident.

> 'On our arrival at San Carlos we were required to submit to customs-house regulations, the officer insisting upon searching our trunks. To this we demurred, having passed through the entire country without submitting to such an ordeal. The officer seeming anxious to compromise the matter, demanded $5 instead from each; the Americans who had preceded us submitted to this extortion, but we were determined to resist. The officer became more moderate coming down–down– down-to a real; upon our refusing to pay this, he made a move in the direction of the cannon which was near; we, however, were first to possess it, and things for a moment wore a warlike appearance. The officer, not wishing to bring things to a crisis, held a consultation with our 'Padrone,' and came to the conclusion that all was right, that as we were Americans he would treat us with due consideration.'

These groups were some of the last to travel the San Juan independently and Letts's party actually passed Vanderbilt's little steamer, The Director, on its way upstream to start the river and lake service.

Chapter 21   Vanderbilt and Isthmus Traffic

The arrival of the steamships and the first regular passenger ship in 1851, the stern wheeler the Sir Henry Bulwer, took much of the business of the bongos, but it still took six days to reach San Carlos after heroic battles through the rapids.   Vanderbilt already had a double side-wheeler, the 120 ton Director in the lake, where after a perilous trip up the river when she had to be hauled over the El Diablo rapids she became the first lake steamer.   To preserve his ships, Vanderbilt had the Bulwer plying Greytown to El Castillo and the Director, El Castillo to Granada; neither ship having to face the El Diablo rapids.

Vanderbilt now had ships connecting all the way from New York to San Francisco and on his return to Greytown from New York, boarded the Bulwer to head upriver.   He had decided that La Virgen to San Juan del Sur was the best land route from the lake to the Pacific and wanted to oversee its inauguration.   One hour out from Greytown and the Bulwer was stuck on a sandbank, everyone on board was helping but no amount of pushing and pulling would free her. To no avail, she was stuck fast.   The cavalry came in the guise of the British Navy who with chains, power and brawn got the Bulwer on her way with steam up, wheel churning, smoke belching and cheers from both sides; an uncommon act of camaraderie at this period of time.   This was the dry season and the Machuca rapids were very dangerous and the ship was forced back by the current every time she tried to get through.   Vanderbilt in some exasperation took charge, tied the safety valve down and, raising as much steam as he could, headed the ship into the rapids, close to shore. Straining every seam, the ship creaking and shuddering, it slowly inched forward until the boat could no longer gain against the current and she came to a stop.   More steam and very slowly she again crept upstream; she hit and slid around rocks, tree trunks swept downstream slammed into her and she also had to avoid the wreck of the Orus. Vanderbilt had brought the Orus to the San Juan the year before and although he had tried to make the river easier to navigate by blasting some of the rocks, she had been swept down the rapids and her remains are still visible today. Three hours later and the Bulwer was through and on its way to El Castillo. El Diablo proved impossible and the Bulwer was abandoned. Vanderbilt, passengers and luggage were all transferred to the faithful bongos to meet the Director upstream and above the rapids for the last stretch of the river and the trip across the lake which was:

'….running as high as an angry Atlantic'.

The route boomed and more steamers were brought to the San Juan. Vanderbilt had now divided the waterway into four sections for the dry season. There were two new steamers on the lake that plied between La Virgen and the El Toro rapids, the Bulwer between the rapids and El Castillo, The Director taking the section from El Castillo to the Machuca and then others for the final leg to Greytown. The bongo came into its own again on the sand bar filled section of the river between the Rio Colorado and Greytown after steamers became stranded, sometimes all night, when there was often rain and always mosquitoes.

To get around the rapids everything had to be portaged and transferred from ship to ship irrespective of weather and class. During the wet season El Diablo was the only unpassable section but in the dry season the whole process was repeated at each set of rapids, the passengers having to walk along the bank, their experiences quite different.

'....the path overhung by the beautiful foliage of the tall trees,...and studded on one side by the dense and to me, novel and interesting undergrowth.....the walk adds an agreeable variety to the journey'.

Whilst another traveller remembers:

'...we had to walk two and a half miles around the (Machuca) rapids through the worst road or path you ever saw, mud very deep and sticky, it took all day.'

Enterprising Indians had opened small bars with refreshments at both ends of the rapids and even though they charged exorbitant prices, they were well frequented.

By 1852 the trip from Greytown to La Virgen was down to three days. In 1853 a new dock and offices were built at Punta Arenas which meant that passengers could transfer directly from the ocean going ship to the river steamer, which might be carrying as many as 600 to 1000 passengers. By 1854 the trip was taking 25 hours, all ships were filled to capacity with three steamers on the long run to the Machuca rapids. The ships were crowded, there were no facilities, no privacy, little chance to sleep, often wet and at night, mosquitoes.

By 1855 there were more passengers than the steamers could carry and Vanderbilt had to do something about the situation as Panama had opened a railway across the isthmus and this route was gaining popularity. He added yet two more ships, the Colorado and the San Carlos to his fleet. They had shallow drafts and the Colorado had room for 1000 passengers whilst the San Carlos, which was 250 feet long, held 1500, had state rooms and a dining room, bunks and drinking water. The only portage now was at El Diablo and even the cost of baggage had been lowered as it was carried in rail cars pulled along the tracks by mules. Should the steamers go aground there were poles to push them off and ropes to help pull them up the rapids. From Greytown to San Juan del Sur, using stagecoaches for the last, land part of the trip, it took 21½ hours, less time than it takes today.

The town of El Castillo was thriving, as it was the one stopping place on the river where the passengers had time on their hands. Hundreds of passengers were milling about waiting for transport in one direction or the other. The railway was working and there was a bustle of ships loading and unloading. About 200 people, mainly Americans had opened bars, restaurants, shops, hotels and dormitories. Every building had something to sell and one passenger remarked:

'…it is safe to say that everything in Castillo is for sale'.

The town was squeezed between the river and the hill and all this activity was crushed into that confined space.

Mark Twain travelled the route on a large comfortable steamer to San Carlos and then transferred to a more crowded double-decker stern-wheeler, but with it's shallow draft it was able to travel the whole river in the wet season. As always, it was left to the forest, the birds and alligators to provide the entertainment. One traveller commented that:

'huge alligators lay and sunned themselves and slept; birds with gaudy feathers and villainous hooked bills stood stupidly on overhanging boughs, and startled one suddenly out of his long cherished, dimly-defined notion that that sort of bird only lived in menageries.'

Other passengers idly took pot-shots at this wildlife.

At night they would tie up for the night and Twain recounts:

'Those who had hammocks swung them, and those who hadn't made beds of their overcoats, and soon the two dingy lanterns, hung forward and aft, shed a ghostly glimmer over the thick-strewn and vaguely defined multitude of slumberers.'

Next morning any discomfort was forgiven when a breakfast of coffee, tea, sandwiches and cheese appeared and when Greytown was reached it was described as a:

'...very pretty little village....all white paint and green leaves and wavy palm trees'.

The exit to the ocean was now very perilous and the bar almost closed. Although dredging had started in the silt-choked harbour, the passengers had to be ferried to and from their ships that were anchored nearly one mile out to sea, not infrequently capsizing into water full of sharks patrolling the bay.

Belt, who travelled upriver a couple of years later than Twain wrote, on reaching San Carlos:

'It was too dark when we arrived at San Carlos to see anything that night of the great lake, but we heard the waves breaking on the beach as on a sea-shore... slept on board one of the steamers of the American Transit Company....built expressly for shallow water. The bottom is quite flat..., the first deck being only about 18 inches above the water...Above this are placed the cargo. A second deck is for passengers about 7 inches above the first. Above this another deck on which are the cabins of the officers and the steering apparatus. The appearance of such a structure is more like that of a house than a boat. The one we were in drew only three feet of water when laden with 400 passengers and twenty tons of cargo.'

As daylight broke next morning:

'To the north-west a great sheet of quiet water extended as far as the eye could reach, with islands here and there, and the great conical peak of Omotepec towered up.'

That evening after a day sailing across the lake, sometimes becalmed:

'About noon the wind failed, and the sun right overhead, in a clear pitiless sky, scorched us with its rays, while our boat lay like a log upon the water, the pitch melting in the seams with the heat.' 'One of the islands is a favourite sleeping place for the white egrets. From all sides they were flying across the lake towards it; and as night set in, the trees and bushes by the water-side were full of them, gleaming like great white flowers amongst the dark green foliage. Flocks of muscovy and whistling ducks also flew to their evening feeding-places. Great masses of a floating plant shaped like a cabbage, were abundant on the lake, and on these the white egrets and other wading birds often alighted.'

'The boatmen told me, and the story is likely enough to be true, that the alligators, floating about like logs, with their eyes above the water, watch these birds, and moving quietly up until within a few yards of them, sink down below the surface, come up underneath them, catch them by the legs and drag them underwater.'

'Besides the alligators, large freshwater sharks appear to be common in the lake.'

That night they arrived at San Ubaldo, Belt's base for his trip to the gold mine.

Chapter 22   The Decline of the River

La Virgen on Lake Cocibolca and San Juan del Sur on the Pacific, the two towns at either end of the land section of the isthmus route were expanding whilst San Carlos, where the ships stopped only briefly, saw little progress, even though it and its fort presided over the whole route. The river was at its most prosperous and its decline was inevitable.

The 1850s had been turbulent on the river as the whole Walker fracas coincided with the river transport expansion and the toll on the ships was great. Troops would take command of any available ship at will, and at least 22 were lost on the waterway with very little in the way of remains to be seen today. The transit company had no lack of passengers but finding suitable boats was another matter and the final straw, or rather nail, for the transit company, was the completion of the trans US railway, which in a single blow rang the death knell of the transit route. The ships that had been bought for the lake steamer service, including the Victoria, 136 feet long and 28 feet wide, became a lake ferry boat that travelled between Granada and San Carlos, stopping at towns on the way, including San Jorge which had by now taken over from La Virgen as the western lake port.

Towards the end of the 1800s the lake was still stormy as rebellious forces and government troops were using it to transfer troops to aid Nicaragua in its war with Honduras, while government troops also used it to transport troops to take the Mosquito coast. But the waterway services and facilities were becoming less and less until there was only one boat every four days or so from Granada to Greytown, about the same service as today.

In 1899 there was an attempt to use the river to oust President Zelaya but troops sent down the river soon put a stop to that though it did result in refurbished forts at El Castillo and San Carlos. Zelaya was to be very thankful for this when, in 1903 Emmiliano Chamorro who was a long-time adversary of Zelaya, organised an uprising. The Victoria was captured, then an armed lake steamer and after men had been picked up from Zapatera and other islands, Chamorro headed for San Carlos. His first attempt to take the fort failed but at the second, he found the fort empty and took possession of it and the positions on Zapatera and Omotepe islands. But Zelaya had not been idle, and in a brief battle he re-took the Victoria and Chamorro fled, an episode known as the 'Revolution of the Lake'. Six years later Chamorro was again on the river this time aiding a revolt by General Estrada but, although they had some success, were defeated and fled into the jungle.

In 1905 Britain signed a treaty relinquishing possession of the mosquito coast. By then the navigation company had been bought by the Nicaraguan government and Greytown was no longer a Freeport.

Chapter 23   Canals

The Panama land route was a huge success evidenced by the sheer quantity of treasure it carried, not only from Panama but also from Colombia, Peru and elsewhere, and affirmed by Spain's refusal to allow any other route across the isthmus, but even they were thinking of a water route.

The first real proposal to construct a canal across the land bridge was in 1551 by Lopez de Gomara to Charles V of Spain:

'For the glory of Spain.'

The King started to look into the idea of a canal across Panama but the report he received stated:

'....that the obstacles to be overcome were so great that even the resources of the most powerful monarch were not adequate for the purpose'.

It was also recorded that, after discussions with his religious advisers, he decided that if there was meant to be a canal joining the two oceans, God would have put it there. For whatever reason, the idea was abandoned.

Another survey was conducted for a Nicaraguan canal, but that was also unfavourable and it was more than 200 years later, in 1781, that saw what was probably the first serious proposal for a waterway across the isthmus, up the Rio San Juan across Lake Cocibolca and then a canal to the Pacific.   At this time the depth of the lake was not known, there was no knowledge about how locks worked, and the idea quickly lost its attraction when the surveyor concluded that, as the lake was 134 feet above sea level, if an access to the Pacific was to exist, both the lake and the river would just drain into the sea.

By the 1800s Britain had business and political dealings in Central America and the United States was getting worried. In 1823 President James Monroe drafted a doctrine to try to contain the expansionism. It referred to the European Powers and included:

'...to declare that we should consider any attempt on their part to extend their system to any portion of this hemisphere as dangerous to our peace and safety.'

The Doctrine was described by the President in very precise terms:

'The occasion has been adjudged proper for asserting as a principle in which the rights and interests of the United States are involved, that the American Continents, by the free and independent condition which they have assumed and maintained, are henceforth not to be considered as subjects for future colonization by any European powers.'

Hugh Gordon Miller who had been Assistant United State Attorney made, in 1929, the following comment on the doctrine:

'No free state in the Americas was to be used by Europeans for colonization. None was to be treated as a 'springboard' from which a European power could land on our shores'

The United States was setting up trading posts along the Pacific coast for merchants who were shipping goods between America and the expanding markets in the Far East and for whalers who were working in Pacific waters; they both needed a route to get their goods from the Pacific to the eastern United States. Besides North America, Britain, France and Holland were all attracted by the idea of a canal. Surveys followed and a feasibility study was produced, even though one of the organisers and most of the workers died of yellow fever. In 1825 an American canal company was formed but its backers eventually decided that it was too risky. President Jackson sent Charles Biddle to negotiate terms under which a canal could be built but he was recalled to Washington in disgrace after it was discovered that he had found it just too tempting and was negotiating a personal contract for himself to build the canal. In 1835 the president of the Federacion Centroamericana charged the English engineer John Baily to provide the first professional report, a feasibility study for a canal that even suggested a tunnel for part of the way. But the Federation collapsed, the recommendations were not implemented, and the president was out of a job.

In the 1840s Britain was trying to keep some control over any Nicaraguan canal. They had recognised the Misquito kingdom and had seized San Juan de Norte at the mouth of the San Juan and asserted:

'The territory of the Misquito Indians included the port of San Juan de Nicaragua which would be the terminus of any canal that should be cut across Nicaragua. As the Misquitos were held to be a kingdom under the protection of Great Britain, the bearing of the claim on their behalf was obvious.'

Britain had its Atlantic base, from where she could block any canal project of which she did not approve, and there were rumours emerging from England that she was looking for a Pacific outlet. In 1847 both the United States and Colombia thought that Britain was trying to acquire Panama. The zealous United States representative in Colombia, Benjamin Bidlack, had instructions to hinder any attempt by any other power to gain any special rights in Panama. To keep any threat of Britain at bay, he negotiated a treaty with Colombia (which then included Panama) in which the United States guaranteed the rights of transit across the isthmus and Colombia would have control over the area. In return the United States was guaranteed free access to any future canal. This historic treaty was sent to the president James K. Polk who advised his senate that if it was not signed, then Britain would step in and take over the isthmus. It took another year and a half before the senate signed but from then on the United States took on the responsibility for the isthmus.

The race was on and in 1848 Costa Rica had designs on Nicaraguan territory and was surveying one route and France was interested. Napoleon had faith in the future of Nicaragua and had, himself, suggested a route through lakes Cocibolca and Managua to the northwest Pacific coast.

> '...a state as admirably situated as Constantinople, and, we must say, up to this time as uselessly occupied. We allude to the State of Nicaragua. As Constantinople is the centre of the ancient world, so is the town of León the centre of the new and, if the tongue of land which separates its two lakes from the Pacific Ocean were cut

through, she would command by virtue of her central position, the entire coast of North and South America. The State of Nicaragua can become, better than Constantinople, the necessary route of the great commerce of the world, and is destined to attain an extraordinary degree of prosperity and grandeur.'

Everything suddenly became all the more urgent when gold was found that year in California.

Britain wanted a canal to speed its trade with its eastern colonies; its trade with Australia alone was worth $200 million and an easier route with more favourable winds and climate would be welcome.

The United States was doing everything it could to prevent Britain from having any part of the isthmus trade routes and trying to get absolute control for itself.

'Under no circumstances would the United States permit Great Britain or any other power to exercise exclusive control of any isthmian transit route.'

The United States tried to negotiate with Britain but with very little success, but they held a trump card. They had negotiated treaties with Nicaragua and Honduras giving Washington exclusive rights to build any canal in those countries, though it was never ratified. Squier was sent from the United States to prepare the way for the clang and noise of the great steamers as they travelled a canal that would run from ocean to ocean.

He was scathing about what he found in Greytown and about the Mosquito Kingdom. That Britain had seized the port under the:

'...shallow pretext of supporting...the mosquitoes, and in virtue of some equivocal relations which the pirates of Jamaica anciently maintained with them even though no mosquito Indian ever resided here ...even though Britain asserted that its sole design in taking the step was the re-establishment of Mosquito rights and authority, Her Britannic Majesty's Consul...is, in fact, dictator of the place. There are no written laws or regulations and an English flag floats over the customs house. If this port belongs to the suppostitious Mosquito King, it is difficult to understand how a second party can exercise sovereignty over it. The thing is too absurd to be continued.'

Perhaps his vehemence was in part due to the fact that:

'Nearly all the imports and exports of Nicaragua, and a considerable part of those of Costa Rica, pass through here; and here also reside the agents of the foreign houses engaged in trade with this portion of the continent. In fact, so far as commercial facilities are concerned, it is far the most important point between New Granada and Mexico.'

Another letter, from a different source, to the United States President stated that:

'The object of Great Britain in the seizure is evident from the policy which she has uniformly pursued throughout her history, of seizing upon every valuable commercial port in the world, whenever circumstances have placed it in her power. Her purpose, probably is to obtain the control of the route for a railroad and canal between the

Atlantic and the Pacific oceans, by way of Lake Nicaragua.'

Vanderbilt wanted a charter to build a canal but the government of Nicaragua was fed up with earlier failed projects and would not listen to him but Squier agreed to his proposition and it was signed and ratified in 1849.

Discussions continued but Great Britain had realised that the United States wished to build, operate and own any canal solely, completely and totally. The way through the intransigent positions of Mr. Clayton and Lord Palmerston came when it was conceded that:

'..neither power actually sought monopoly power over the canal, the way was cleared of the most formidable obstacle to the conclusion of a treaty.'

The final Clayton-Bulwer treaty of 1850 gave both nations a share in the canal and stated that:

'The United States of America and Her Britannic Majesty, being desirous of consolidating the relations of amity which so happily subsit between them, by setting forth and fixing in a convention their views and intentions with reference to any means of communication by ship-canal which may be constructed between the Atlantic and Pacific Oceans by the way of the river San Juan de Nicaragua and either or both of the lakes of Nicaragua or Managua, to any port or place on the Pacific Ocean.'

And more pertinent:

'The Governments of the United States and Great Britain hereby declare that neither the one nor the other will ever obtain or maintain for itself any exclusive control over the said ship canal...'

There were clauses that offered joint terms to Great Britain on the building of a canal, the protection of any canal and the rights of commerce and navigation; that two free ports would be established, one at each end, and that they would not

'occupy, or fortify, or colonize, or exercise any dominion over Nicaragua, Costa Rica, the Misquito Coast or any part of Central America.'

Although some of this last phrase included Nicaragua, it was clear that it referred to any potential isthmus route, something that was to be of enormous importance later with the United States involvement with the Panama Canal.

The senate greeted the treaty with considerable anger that Great Britain was equal partners with the United States when building any isthmus canal. The British in return agreed to withdraw from San Juan de Nicaragua and renounced their protectorate on the Atlantic Coast and, kept the peace.

Vanderbilt had commissioned a survey of the river in 1850 by the American Atlantic and Pacific Ship Canal Company, with a view to building a canal at an estimated cost was $32 million. Britain had let it be known that capital might be forthcoming to help finance such a project so Vanderbilt set off for London, and her bankers, but they refused to help on the grounds that the costs were excessive.

Vanderbilt abandoned the canal idea and concentrated on his waterway business.

Walker and Vanderbilt were squabbling and Nicaragua was fighting its National War so, for business, Panama was looking better all the time. A trans-Panama railway had been built, but at a cost of 9,000 lives:

'…a life for every railway tie'.

After it opened, 750 million US dollars worth of gold travelled along it during the first fourteen years. Then, in 1878, France entered the scene. Ferdinand de Lesseps was the builder of the Suez Canal and he declared that he was going to build a Panama Canal. The United States stated that they would never agree to a non-US controlled canal and warships were dispatched. With gallic disregard, de Lesseps started digging to try to repeat the success he had had with the Suez Canal. However, using the same system, it just did not work; rock and mud falling back into the cut. Six years later he returned to France, bankrupt, and where both he and his son faced court charges of fraud and bribery. He left behind a bit of a canal and 20,000 dead men, many from disease; malaria, dysentery and yellow fever, some knowing that they had such a high chance of dying, that they even brought their own coffins with them. The description of their conditions is horrific:

'…"a foul hole…toilets are quite unknown, all the rubbish is thrown into the swamps or onto rubbish heaps. Toads splash in the liquid muck…rats infest the solid filth…snakes hunt both toads and rats; clouds of mosquitoes swarm into the houses.'

Other studies were undertaken by the United States, one in 1885 about a possible Nicaraguan route included a young Robert E. Peary, the first man to the North Pole, and a Cuban engineer who, in his report stated:

'...that the route herein described...is perfectly practical, free of engineering complications and problems and is, in addition, the most economic, convenient and secure for a maritime link between the Atlantic and the Pacific, not only across Nicaragua but across any other part of the American isthmus.'

He also suggested that a canal be built to run parallel to the San Juan river on the north bank for the last stretch as the river as the river became so swollen with water in the rainy season from the Sarapiqui and the San Carlos Rivers that it would avoid sedimentation and would exit at the lagoon at San Juan de Nicaragua. The cost, about $50 million.

The next detailed design for a Nicaraguan Canal was put forward towards the end of the 1800s. The work would be extensive as the following, much shortened, summary will give an idea.

'At Fort San Carlos, the outlet of the lake into the San Juan river a large amount of bottom dredging will be necessary. This is through soft mud and the engineers have reported that it is entirely feasible. A great dam will be constructed 64 ½ miles from the lake at Ochoa, just above the Machodo river, which will make the river the same summit level as that of the lake. This will give navigation the whole distance from the Ochoa dam into and across the lake. From Ochoa the river is tortuous and shallow and will no longer be followed. The canal will be constructed north of the river through the valleys of the San Francisco and the Deceado rivers, in which valleys great basins will be formed by large embankments; the sea level being reached by three locks.

On the western side it will require 17 ¼ miles of canal from the shores of the lake to the port of Brito on the Pacific. The canal will go through a great depression in the valley of the Tola, which, by means of a dam, will furnish a basin of water of 4,000 acres with a width of 13,000 feet. There will be three locks upon this side, as there are upon the Atlantic side, the greatest of which will be 650 feet long, eighty feet wide and with a lift of 45 feet. Between the last lock on the Pacific side and Brito, the canal will be used as an enlarged part of the harbour. In short, the Nicaraguan canal will consist of the great basin of the lake connected with the Atlantic ocean by the San Juan river, excavated canal work and the Tola basin on the side of the Pacific.

Little dredging is necessary in the lake. At Greytown, a 1,700 feet jetty to be constructed into the ocean. The Ochoa dam is 1,200 feet in length, 70 feet high and constructed by dumping rocks, the gaps will fill up with debris and form a natural bed. Weirs will take the overflow water. In the Deceado valley the embankment will be 70 feet high and 1,035 feet wide to form a basin three miles long and between 30 and 70 feet deep. In addition there will be two other basins where ships can rest, make repairs and pass each other at speed safely.

At The Great Divide Cut on the eastern end, the canal to be cut three miles through rock averaging 140 feet with a maximum of 320 feet and the removal of 12,000,000 feet of rock, to be used in the Ochoa dam, and to a depth of 30 feet.

Rio San Juan

Ocean to ocean 169 1/4miles with free navigation of 142 ½ miles will take about 28 hours.'

It was not until 1889 that construction was started by the Maritime Canal Company of Nicaragua of a fifteen mile canal from Greytown to a point on the San Juan between San Carlos and the Sarapiqui river. A breakwater was built out to sea to allow ocean-going ships to enter the harbour once again and six dredges were brought to start work excavating the canal. An eleven mile railroad was built to convey people and construction materials and four miles of canal were dug. In 1893 everything came to an end through lack of financial backing and all that is visible of the enterprise today is the decaying dredge and some tenders in the lagoon near New Greytown.

A final review was undertaken in 1897 when the cost of a canal with ten locks, a dam across the San Juan where the San Carlos runs into it and a 100 miles of railway to facilitate building was US$118 million.

The next event of significance was the annexation of Hawaii in 1893 and the building of the first giant battleships. Their only route to the eastern seaboard of the United States was around Cape Horn. During the Spanish/American war in 1898 it took the battleship Oregon 67 days to navigate from the west coast of the USA to Cuba. The push for a canal was truly on, and a side-event, saved the lives of millions worldwide.

Malaria and yellow fever were the two deadliest dangers that plagued Central America and the Caribbean, including Cuba, where yellow fever was endemic and from where it had spread to North America. Hundreds of thousands of people had died from the two diseases with yellow fever the most deadly and feared. Accounts of deaths are numerous: a force sent by Napoleon to Haiti in 1800 was completely destroyed. Whole villages and boat crews would succumb and in 1726 an expedition to wipe out pirates lost 4,000 men from a total of 4,750. Before the United States became a nation, 100,000 people had died, in 1792 one tenth of the population of Philadelphia had fallen victim and of one force of 1,500 US soldiers, 1,400 men had expired. When the American Spanish war came to an end in 1898 the United States forces occupied areas that were badly affected with yellow fever and, one year later, of every 1,000 troops, 600 were sick.

In 1848 it had been suggested, for the first time, that perhaps mosquitoes were the carrier and in 1881 a Cuban doctor carried out some experiments, but being restricted by the knowledge available at that time he could not show an actual case of transmission. Research proceeded to determine the cause of malaria and it was discovered that the disease was caused by a parasite and that the mosquito was the transmitter and intermediate host.

There was an all-out attempt to try to control malaria, Sir Ronald Ross received the Nobel prize for his work during 1895-1899 that advocated:

> '...the use of screens to keep mosquitoes out, the clearing away of all rubbish, killing mosquitoes by fumigations, oiling all stagnant waters, the drainage of swamps and the filling in of all pools and puddles'.

In Cuba, the Chief Sanitary Officer, Surgeon General William Gorgas, who, at this time, did not believe in the mosquito theory, was zealously cleaning Havana as he thought that dirt and filth could be responsible for causing the disease. One report by him stated:

'...the present opinion is that one has not to contend with an organism or germ which may be taken into the body with food or drink, but with an almost inexplicable poison so insidious in its approach and entrance that no trace is left behind.'

The possibility of building a canal in one of the areas worst infected by yellow fever may have been instrumental in the setting up of a commission in 1900 to try to determine what caused the disease and how it was transmitted. One of the members, Major Walter Reed, was highly respected and known as a brilliant and resourceful bacteriologist. He proceeded to Havana, which by now was probably the cleanest city in the world, but there were more cases of yellow fever than ever. It was already apparent that the disease was not caught through contact between people, healthy men had slept on the sheets and blankets of sufferers and not caught the disease. It was on a visit to a barracks that Reed realised that the yellow fever sufferers had all been bitten by one or more mosquitoes.

The only way to prove that mosquitoes were the carriers was by experiment and as yellow fever was unknown in animals, the guinea pigs had to be human. The following account is the story of the experiment as recorded in the American Association for Medical Progress.

'Volunteers were called for and the Commissioners insisted that they themselves should be included. Every man knew that he was likely to die, but he also knew that in so dying he might save thousands of his fellow men from death. The volunteers, who refused to accept any reward except for a small government pension, allowed themselves to be bitten by mosquitoes which had previously bitten yellow fever patients. Lazear (one of the commissioners) was one of the first, and he soon became ill with yellow fever and died in convulsions. Carroll (another commissioner) almost died; for three days his life hung in the balance.

The experiment was continued on eleven other men, and as nine of them contracted yellow fever, Reed felt justified in saying that the disease was carried by mosquitoes.'

But, not everyone was convinced and Reed arranged for a second, conclusive, experiment to take place. It was held under strict scientific conditions, away from other human habitation and the building kept under armed guard.

'A mosquito-screened building was erected and divided into two apartments. One man was put into each apartment where they remained until the researchers were confident that both men were healthy. Then one of the men had fifteen mosquitoes that had previously bitten yellow fever patients introduced into his apartment, where they all proceeded to bite him. In four days he became ill with yellow fever. The, now two men, in the other apartment remained healthy. As a final test, the mosquitoes were all removed from the apartment, which was also disinfected, and another man placed inside and whom remained healthy.'

The link between mosquito and yellow fever was proven and, like malaria, the disease was caused by a parasite. Reed had wanted to volunteer along with the other commissioners but he was refused as being too old; two years later he died of appendicitis.

Havana was put under siege to destroy the mosquitoes and their breeding grounds and for the first time in 140 years, there were no cases of yellow fever.

The United States was now determined to get a canal built and it would be totally controlled by the United States. They realised that any canal would dominate the region as it would become the 'jugular vein' of North and South America and its political control would always be of vital concern to the United States. Nicaragua was considered but President Roosevelt thought it too shallow and Panama became the favourite. De Lesseps had already started building a canal but he had been bought out by a French company, who were now asking US$109 million. The cost was too high and Nicaragua's lakes and rivers, again, became the first choice.

The Panama Canal Company now had a new agent, a smooth talking lawyer, William Nelson Cromwell who was aided by a brilliant engineer Buneau-Varilla, a major shareholder in the canal company who was trying to move everything along very quickly as the Colombian concession expired in 1903. Supported by Roosevelt they launched the campaign for a Panamanian canal. Cromwell was described as a financial wizard and:

'...has an intellect that works like a flash of lightning, and it swings about with the agility of an acrobat.'

He now used some of these skills to persuade the French to reduce their price to US$40million. No-one knows how much money was spent to try to achieve this as there were suspicions of fraud. US$60,000 from the canal fund was used by one senator to help the Republican party's presidential campaign, which gives some indication of the amounts of money involved and available, though the $60,000 was later returned together with a one million dollar 'fee'. Cromwell later burnt most of the papers relating to the Panama Canal project and his partners, one of whom was John Foster Dulles, destroyed the rest.

Then nature stepped in to give Panama a helping hand when a volcano erupted on Martinique in the Caribbean destroying a city of 30,000 people, burying it in lava. All the senators were informed that Nicaragua had similar volcanoes and that the same thing could happen there. Mombotombo had erupted only a few months earlier and Nicaragua had produced its famous postage stamp showing the erupting volcano. One of these was placed on every senator's desk and hanging on a wall was a 20 foot long map of Central America with red and black dots, active and dormant volcanoes. Nicaragua had lots of dots.

The combination of a cheap, partly built canal and the fact that all the ships on any Nicaraguan canal route would have to pass by Omotepe and its volcanoes and President Zelaya's insistence that no single country would be allowed to finance any canal project and that the canal would remain Nicaraguan, as only Nicaragua could have sovereignty over a canal in its own country: Panama got the vote. It was made law in 1901.

As a post-script, Zelaya, who was talking with the British about a railway across the isthmus was arrested by the US after a show of strength by US marines who landed at Bluefields. Even later, when the Panama canal opened in 1914 Washington was still manoeuvring and managed to get Nicaragua to give the United States exclusive rights, in perpetuity, to build a canal through Nicaragua, in exchange for US$3 million debt relief. It took until 1970 to get this revoked.

The idea of a canal resurfaces occasionally in Nicaragua and a deep draft canal was suggested in 1929 and a shallow draft canal in 1939. The Japanese proposed a huge canal that would allow ships four times larger than those of the Panama Canal but that was during the Sandanista/Contra war when a canal was not top of the agenda. Even now a group of business men are trying to find support for a new look at the idea. Nicaragua would welcome the revenues but while the canal is only a dream what Nicaragua does have is a glorious, unspoilt river, one of the most untouched rainforests in the world, huge lakes and the mysterious islands of Zapatera, Omotepe and Solentiname.

Chapter 24   Up the River and Solentiname

Our ferry boat back to San Carlos was a lancha, a modern fibre-glassed version of the bongo, it was about 30 feet long and seven feet wide and had all the same problems in the dry season as the bongo's had.   It held some 60 passengers with luggage, and cargo and with two big outboard motors took eleven hours to San Carlos from New Greytown, or nine hours downriver.

We relaxed and watched the scenery whilst the two powerful engines pushed us upriver.   The Machuca rapids were taken very carefully and the engines raised so that the propellers were barely in the water and less likely to crunch into any rocks.   Only when well clear of any hazards were they allowed to dig deeper into the water and speed us on. We stopped for petrol, more snacks and drinks and a short walk, with the compulsory parrot, in a garden teaming with flowers and hummingbirds.   One thing that you do not have to worry about on this trip is starvation, and later on when we slowed in the river a canoe immediately took off from the river-bank towards us.   Hot chicken, beans, rice, salad, platano and cheese served on a paper plate with a fork for about two dollars.   No one threw their plates, forks and cups into the river but conscientiously used the plastic rubbish bags put out for the purpose.

Twelve hours after leaving New Greytown we were in San Carlos.   Joe decided that it was easier to load everything into the canoe and drive it around the bay to the hotel.   There was no choice but to spend another night in San Carlos.

San Carlos is gorgeously situated, the view from the citadel in the town or from one of lakeside bars over the lake towards the islands and the peaks of Omotepe to the right and the entrances to the San Juan and Frio rivers to the left is magnificent. Squier called it:

'...one of the finest views in the world'.

He described hundreds of sunning alligators on the sand bar between the two rivers, today, the site of a fishing lodge. We watched birds streaming up the river and across the lake to their roosts the sight breathtaking against the setting sun.

Next morning, our adventure was over, the car was packed and the canoe on top, nestled on its mattress. We headed out to breakfast at the bus station. We drove slowly along the waterfront, mainly to avoid being run over by crazy taxi drivers, when a shout of "Joe, Joe Brown!" brought us to a halt. There, by the ferry to Solentiname was a friend of ours from Granada, Roberto. A good-looking middle-aged Nicaraguan, he and Joe had talked about going down the San Juan and we knew that he had a house on one of the Solentiname islands. He was just going out to the house on the ferry later that day and why didn't we go with him? We all headed for breakfast and, with Roberto accompanying us, the service was instant.

Roberto was in the process of transforming his house into a hotel. He said that he had plenty of space and why didn't we go and stay with him for three days until the ferry returned to San Carlos? We had no reason to go rushing back to Granada, and we did want to see the Solentiname islands. Getting to San Carlos was the hard bit, getting to the islands was easy. Three more days wouldn't make much difference.

Back to the car, we unpacked everything again and, picking our way around fish vendors, broken concrete with coarse dusty grass poking through the cracks, mangy dogs and broken steps, transferred everything to the Solentiname ferry-boat and tied the canoe on top. A quick trip to the market for some essentials, a mound of rice and beans and cheese, large jugs of water, a couple of coolers with perishable stuff, some vegetables and coffee. Rolls of barbed wire, a water pump that had been in town for repair, bags of cement and other essential building materials. It suddenly dawned, bright and clear, we were going to another building site!

The loaded ferry eventually left the dock in San Carlos and headed out between a narrow but clearly marked channel that led to the islands. Off to the west we saw the island of Zapote, the largest bird-nesting site in Nicaragua. In front and beyond the islands of Solentiname we just glimpsed the evocative peaks of Omotepe.

Solentiname is an oasis about which we knew very little. It lies 17 kilometres from San Carlos and has 36 islands. There is a twice-weekly ferry service, no airstrip, no cars, no roads, no electricity and no water system. The islands used to be covered with forest but, as they were conveniently situated on the lake between San Carlos and La Virgen, most of the trees were cut when the steamships changed from coal burning to wood burning. Other trees were cut for carpentry but all commercial cutting stopped 30 years ago. However, legal or not, balsa trees (of Kon Tiki fame) are cut, but others planted, to support a local industry making carved birds, fish and other animals. The balsa tree is important in the regeneration of forest and as a pioneer species as it is very fast growing and its large leaves provide cover and protection for other plants and is favoured by the howler monkeys. The flowers are huge as, too, are the seedpods. About 10 inches long, the seeds nestle amongst a bed of silky soft kapok; excellent for cushion filler.

Rio San Juan

Balsa trees are harvested young, between five and seven years old as, after this age they develop a taproot and a dark red centre, waterheart, from which, when pierced, water will spurt but it makes the wood too hard for any commercial use. Balsa has been used for rafts for centuries and during the 2nd World War it had a wide range of uses including airplane struts, military gliders, mine floats and insulation. After the war the demand fell until now, when it has had something of a renaissance, as it is being used for insulation in supertankers against static charges caused by wave action. Hopefully, it will continue to be used by model plane and ship enthusiasts; I well remember cutting out small pieces of balsa wood to make struts for model airplanes.

Solentiname managed to avoid most of the skirmishing that occurred on the lake, except for an insurrection that occurred sometime around 1562 or 3, it remained something of a backwater until 1965 when a trappist monk, Father Ernesto Cardinal, arrived on the islands. Born in 1925 in Granada he studied poetry at Colombia University in the 1940s and entered a Trappist monastery in Gethsemane, Kentucky where he envisioned founding a religious community in Nicaragua. Cardinal became ill, not helped by the strict Trappist regime, and had to leave the monastery. Back in Colombia he completed his studies in 1965 and became a Catholic priest. He returned to Nicaragua and bought a piece of land on Solentiname and became priest to the people of the islands, preaching a radical Christianity, Nicaraguan Liberation Theology, that Christ was the saviour of the poor and he encouraged his flock to take part in the ministration of mass. His interpretation gradually evolved into a political outlook that opposed the Somoza government and in 1977 a group of islanders attacked, and overcame, the military base in San Carlos, the first successful rebel attack by the Sandanista uprising. Somoza, however, retaliated by burning most of the buildings on the islands, forcing people to leave. But when Cardinal became Minister of Culture in the later Sandanista government, he rebuilt much that had been lost.

It was this same Ernesto Cardinal who gave painting lessons to 12 farmers and created an internationally known naïve style of painting of wondrous forest scenes with waterfalls and extravagantly coloured birds. Cardinal himself is a respected painter, and sculptor of subjects with beautiful easy lines. He is a poet and an international celebrity, easily recognised at gatherings by his white shirt and black beret.

Today there are still some families painting and the balsa carving is thriving. The whole town of Mancarron is a hive of activity, everybody seemingly involved in the balsa handcrafts. The trees have to be grown and harvested, dried and cut into smaller pieces and then the animals carved and painted. Sitting outside their houses women and girls, and men and boys taking a break from fishing, can be found carefully carving or transforming the almost white wood into gorgeous brilliant creatures, delicately painting feathers on a bird or scales on a fish.

Forty minutes later and we were amongst the islands. Almost covered with vegetation there were occasional houses and gardens with lawns. We pulled into a jetty where a cooler, some barbed wire, a basket of vegetables, a bottle of water and a gas tank were unloaded, together with a young couple. We were told that the owner led a rather exotic lifestyle living part of the year in Solentiname and the other half in the Azores. The boat took off, almost before the people had stepped ashore, and headed around the island to another stop, at another jetty, where more supplies and people were disembarked. An excited nudge from Roberto that we were next and he and Joe clambered to the front, over people, produce and bags, to sit outside, on the roof. The boat boy started to sort out our stuff and handed it up to Joe and onto the deck ready for our stop. We rounded an island and a garden with lawns and flowers, bushes and trees and a substantial jetty appeared. Roberto's builders were there to meet the boat and we unloaded all our things, the water-pump, supplies, water, propane gas tank for cooking and, of course, the canoe, its engine, fuel tanks, oars, and the big non-waterproof box.

"Arriba, arriba" encouraged Roberto.

He pointed out a steep path and steps that lead to the house. Grabbing a couple of bags each we headed up past flowers and bushes, banana trees, and limes to a large wooden house. Climbing up a somewhat precarious staircase onto a huge veranda; we had arrived. Roberto told us that he bought the island, which had at one time belonged to Somoza, and built the house for his wife. She had designed it and based the design on a much-loved house in which she had lived some years ago in Honduras. Roberto was now converting it into a small hotel with eight bedrooms and bathrooms. The view was stunning, looking over the lake to Padre Island and Mancarron. Roberto unlocked everything and we were shown a large bedroom with huge windows and doors that opened on both sides onto a veranda that ran around the whole house. We wondered why there was no mosquito screening and Roberto told us that, unlike many of the other islands, there were no mosquitoes, which we hopefully believed. He thought that it maybe because he was higher and any breeze just blew them away.

"No snakes either" he remarked.

We went to explore and except for the house and garden the whole island has been left completely undisturbed. At one kilometre long and a quarter wide the forest is a real treasure, a mini habitat. I was very envious of Roberto having his own private jungle. He has now introduced capucin monkeys though I hope they do not get too familiar, they are very clever and very mischievous.

Roberto's message that we were coming had reached the house and tomato salad, rice, beans, cheese, tinned tuna, water, rum and coke were ready for us when we returned. With no electricity, supper was early, as everything had to be washed up and put away before dark. Afterwards we sat in rocking chairs looking out over the lake and chatted, mainly about construction and how to prop up the sagging corner of the house that was in danger of collapsing, until the sun set and night descended. We listened to cicadas, frogs and ghekos, a murmuring in the trees an occasional squeak and howler monkeys on another island and watched fireflies. We were dozing so retreated to bed where we were instantly asleep; and then, as instantly, awake. The entire roof of the house was home to bats. Squeaking incessantly they were zooming through the bedroom, most, thankfully, missing us. They were scrabbling in the roof and on the wire netting. Put up to discourage them it was failing miserably as it just gave them great roosting places. Maybe this was the reason why Roberto did not have many mosquitoes! We thought that we had a bat problem in Granada but it was nothing compared with this. We had insect eating bats living in our roof and had hung dozens of balsa fish and animals from the ceiling, along with fabric hangings, to deter them from flying down the corridors and had put red night-lights in the worse places which had helped, but we never found any way of persuading them to move house. We also had fruit bats, which slept in the palm trees during the day, and were no problem except that they were messy eaters and every morning we had to clean up their dropped pieces of fruit. The smaller insect eating species do keep the insect population down and it was these that were living at Roberto's. We dozed during the night but a pig grunting and then cockerels crowing meant little sleep. At 4.30am we were up making coffee by torchlight and sipping it whilst watching the sunrise.

Roberto emerged seemingly oblivious to the bats. My question about how many pigs he had was met with a puzzled expression.

"We don't have any pigs.'

"Well what was the noise then?"

"Oh that, those are Pato Chancho's".

The pigs turned out to be cormorants and the Spanish name, Pato Chancho translates as pig ducks. We had noticed the wide expanse of white droppings of roosting birds when we had arrived at the jetty and had seen a couple in the trees but that morning we could see that there were hundreds crowded together on the branches.

Fortified by a breakfast of gallopinto (beans and rice), eggs, and cheese, we gathered up some water, biscuits, sunscreen, and petrol and headed out onto an alluring lake. We waved to Roberto, who had had to be left behind to organise his construction workers; sometimes it seemed as though the whole of Nicaragua is building. The water was like glass and we headed from Atrevesada, Roberto's island, past Padre Island from where we had heard the howler monkeys. One pair was introduced a number of years ago and there is now a thriving colony.

The engine disturbed the water and left a fan shape behind us. Like the still days on the river, the only other disturbances were those of the fishes and the diving birds.

The cormorants made a little headfirst dive whilst the anhingas slid backwards and down into the water, both leaving barely a ripple, their heads re-appearing several seconds later.

The islands were beautiful, palm trees, mangoes and balsas, vegetation right down to the water. There were small bays with jetty's and dugout canoes and other wooden boats. Ducks and geese were paddling in the water whilst the customary chickens and pigs scratched and rooted around on the shore. We headed to Mancarron the largest of the islands at 20 square kilometres it is also the highest at 257 metres and named after a sweet palm wine made from the coyol palm. It has a village, a school, a church, a hotel and balsa carvers. The day was so perfect that we decided to just keep going and see as much of the islands as we could and not stop at Mancarron that day. We passed dugout canoes being paddled, a couple with engines and others drifting in the water with fishermen throwing the weighted circular nets or holding lines. We passed a large old ranch house with a wooden chute reaching straight down into the water to load cattle directly into boats. Two women were thigh deep in water washing clothes; their wet skirts clinging to their legs. Children were diving, splashing and climbing onto boats but all stared at us and waved.

Like Omotepe, Solentiname has a range of eco-systems and a wide variety of wildlife, including 46 species of fish. In the early 1900s it was discovered that many of the fish in the lake were rather strange as many species had individuals that were a bright red or coppery gold colour and/or had a large lump on their heads. Some biologists are trying today to find out if there is any advantage to the fish that show these phenomena. The enormous length of waterline is home to birds and along the banks, deer come to drink, as do snakes, and a caiman or crocodile may lurk.

We clung to the banks spotting birds and counting oropendula nests. We edged into a gorgeous bay with palm tress and flowers, herons, cormorants, kingfishers and a flutter of butterflies. Our knowledge of birds tended to be restricted to the big ones, pretty ones and those with an interesting lifestyle so there were many that we couldn't name and, with no binoculars, almost impossible to identify. Next time, we promised ourselves, we will not capsize! On the west side of the bay we saw a small house so we decided to go and investigate. We pulled onto the bank by a cement sink washing area and climbed over some broken rocks to a collapsing wooden house.

"Hola, hola!" we called, but no response. We walked around the house and saw a stony path that meandered up the hill behind.

"Do you think anyone will mind if we walk a little way?'

The path had obviously been used for many years but was now in disrepair and the fruit trees and flowers alongside were rampant. Birds were singing and there was a tangle of trees and creepers ahead. We turned to absorb the view over the lake but not having a machete with us we decided to return to the canoe and continue around the islands. It was hot and super sunny, the light dazzling off the water, the shoreline shimmering in the haze. We covered up in long sleeved shirts, as we were painfully aware that our sunscreen was nothing like strong enough. It was a phenomenal day, though we did not realise that until much later, after Joe on his many return trips, never experienced another day anything like it.

We reached a small, uninhabited, island that had a good beach and a place to escape the sun and where we could have our picnic lunch. We tied onto a tree branch and sat on the bank and watched a group of gorgeously coloured black-winged whistling ducks plopping around in the water under the shade of an overhanging tree. The island was a pile of huge volcanic rocks with plants in every crevice. It was quite impossible to move more than a metre from the beach, machete or no machete. The conversation turned to bats.

"What on earth are we going to do about the bats at Roberto's? One crashed into me last night and I can't sleep." Joe complained

"I know, me too." I replied. "Mosquito nets would help, at the very least it would stop the bats flying into us and keep the mosquitoes out. I know that there are not many mosquitoes, but there are some."

"Perhaps we should just stay up all night and look for fishing bats."

Found in Solentiname, the fishing bat is a very unique animal. It flies over still water at night and by a type of sonar, senses ripples on the water surface. It lowers its feet, with their long claws, into the water and drags them along, through the water, sometimes as far as a metre, by when, whatever it was that alerted the bat, usually a fish, has been caught in the claws. It then flies to a tree, hangs upside down and eats it. Solentiname may have vampire bats too, like Omotepe where they are a real problem. They spend much of their time on the ground and attack the ankles of horses and cattle to feast on the flowing blood.

With no answer to the bat problem and lunch finished we continued around the islands. Suddenly, a lurch and a crunch, the canoe rocked furiously and we came to a complete halt. We had hit a rock and sheared a pin on the propeller. We had a spare so there was no problem, it just had to be replaced but it was hot. We gingerly paddled to the shore, pushing around the larger rocks, until we could get into some shade and tied up. We were at the bottom of a small cliff and at some time the land must have collapsed, tumbling the volcanic rocks into the lake and causing a hazard to shipping. Spare shear pin in place, we set off, took it a bit slower and continued around the corner until we reached open water.

"I just want to go back to the ranch house and talk with them for a moment, if that is OK with you?"

"No problem."

We headed off to the ranch and, with the women and children we had seen in the lake earlier were two men with whom Joe was soon chatting away in his Spanglish. They were telling him about the ranch and that the small house where we had stopped belonged to a priest. Where they were living used to be a big working ranch until recently but now there were no cattle, and they were just living there to keep an eye on everything. Joe had not forgotten about his wooden boat and it turned out that a woman we had seen earlier in the day, rowing a very pretty though old, wooden boat was from the ranch too. We had stopped to talk with her then and Joe had asked her if her boat was for sale. Laughing, she said that her boat was certainly not for sale but that Joe could get one made, just like it, in the village on Mancarron. Lots of waving and 'adios' and we were on our way again. We passed the milk and cheese farm and then the avocado island. We stopped to try to buy some but, apparently, they had all gone to the market.

We saw an anhinga with its wings spread sitting on what looked like a pipe sticking out of the water.

"Better keep clear of that."

"Do you know what I think that is?" says Joe in a sort of surprised, excited, voice.

"I think it is the funnel from one of the lake steamships."

"Surely it would have rotted by now, it would be over an hundred years old." I mused.

Some 43 kilometres later we were back at Roberto's and comparing notes over rum and coke. Roberto's building was coming on well and he was really enthused by the new path and the number of plants that they had put in that day. We were marched off to look and admire them and shown the new, spacious, rooms and we were upbeat about the whole project for him. Solentiname is not easy to get to but there is a flight every day from Managua and, with his own boat at San Carlos to transport people to the island, it would be a fairly quick, interesting and comfortable trip. The fishing is excellent and trophy tarpon waiting to be caught. Roberto hoped that the new road, although not yet started, will bring more tourists and that perhaps some will come from Costa Rica via the Rio Frio and Los Chiles. We hope he does well.

Roberto told us that the ranch we had stopped at was 1,720 manzanas in size but was now in the hands of a bank that wanted to sell it. The problem was that it was very unlikely that it could ever be used to graze cattle again as it had become so overgrown and the grass had been forced out by other plants, but it was fenced. For sale at US$500,000, you could probably buy it for half that. The land with the little wooden shack, he did not know about but was very surprised that a priest might own it. The rocks on which we sheared the pin was one patch, there were others, and to be careful on the outer corners of the islands. Yes, the pipe was part of a steamship though no-one knows which one. This and the few remains that we had passed on the river were all we saw of the busiest time on the waterway. Later we learnt that the remains of thirteen ships are known, one of them very close to our hotel at Sabalos.

The cormorants were beginning to roost and grunting conversationally; and the bats were waking. There are about 200 species of bats in the Central and Southern Americas and in Nicaragua, all its' species seem to be alive and well. No mosquito net, nothing to be done and we just had to try to sleep. Sun and a long day had made us very tired and we spent much of the night unconscious to the bats, though we swept up a pile of droppings in the morning from the floor and off the sheets.

Roberto had already made the coffee by the time we emerged in the morning and was leaning over the balcony listening to excited voices from the vicinity of the dock. A canoe had paddled up and the voices were getting louder and more high-pitched. Roberto was just about to go and find out what was happening when up the path came three of his workers, followed by a good-looking, well-dressed, woman aged about 40 wearing a bright red baseball hat. The main interest though was concentrated on one of the workers who was holding out his machete, like some kind of gift offering, over which was draped a plump 1½ metre long coral snake. So much for no snakes!

"That is the only snake that I have ever seen here." Remarked Roberto.

Now this snake was magnificent, it was banded with lustrous gold, red and black scales, much longer and plumper than any coral snake we had seen before. Of the 70 coral snake species in the Americas, only three are known from Nicaragua and the country only has a total of fourteen species of poisonous snakes. However, the records are not recent and as relatively little research has been done in Nicaragua it is very likely that there are other species waiting to be found.

Snakes have played their role in all the early pre-Colombian religions and the 'feathered serpent' is a familiar symbol. The snake god, the god of wisdom, was one of the seven Inca deities and even today statues of the Virgin Mary with a snake coiled at her feet are common in Central America.

From the days of early exploration, snakes took their toll and they were feared by the early explorers as their bites were often fatal and lurid descriptions were written of symptoms and remedies; bird's beak potions, binding the snake's head to the wound and eating its gall or liver. Plasters of various plants and concoctions of drinks, one, gunpowder, brandy and water. For the ordinary man, often a farmer, the problem is huge. In 1954, 3,000 to 4,000 people are known to have died in Central and South America from snake-bite, and probably the number was much higher as people living in remote areas would be unable to seek treatment and their deaths went unrecorded. In 1998 some 5,000 died in Ecuador from 300,000 people bitten but, again, the numbers may be much higher as in some communities 95% of adult men had been bitten, nearly half more than once, but many of these bites would be from

non-poisonous species. There is very little information about Nicaraguan casualties but about 800 cases are reported each year. One piece of trivia, though not to the person involved, was that the first death in the United States Civil war was a confederate soldier who died after he had been bitten by a coral snake.

When building the Granada house we would come across small coral snakes, a black and white banded variety, which we were assured was very poisonous. Once we had got rid of the piles of old roof tiles, floor tiles and timber, and having found what we thought was the mother, we had not seen any more but you can never be certain that one may not turn up somewhere. All the coral snakes are poisonous to man and many bites are fatal, but all are painful and dangerous. Roberto's snake had been foraging amongst leaf litter around the waters edge where it had, possibly, been looking for eels and fish as a change from its usual diet of other snakes, the most common prey, lizards, other reptiles and amphibia. The workmen were lucky to spot it as they were planting flowers in the area. Their automatic reaction is to kill any snake, harmful or not, and although this snake was potentially extremely dangerous, it was sad to see that such a magnificent animal was dead.

To confuse the situation, a number of perfectly harmless snakes and have the same, or similar, colour patterns of coral snakes. Young boa constrictors have similarly patterned striped tails that they use as a lure to attract attention away from the head. Do not be deceived into thinking that you know the difference between poisonous and non-poisonous species of coral snakes and their mimics as the rhymes that describe the colour patterns as being safe or unsafe, do not always work. Just why some animals mimic the coral snake pattern is quite unclear as any benefit is not obvious. The secondary school teaching, that predators learn that the bright, striped colour pattern belongs to an animal that is dangerous for them to eat so they leave it alone and the non-poisonous mimic benefits by not getting eaten either. Alas, this just does not hold true particularly when some coral snakes take on a melanistic colouration that is similar to harmless snakes.

Birds are one of the most common predators on snakes and it has been possible to show in some, including the Motmot bird, an innate aversion to combinations of the red, black, and yellow stripes of the coral snakes, but other birds could not care less and coral snakes and their mimics, are both eaten indiscriminately. The birds are in danger from a bite from the snakes so, before eating it, they kill it, but seem quite unaffected by the poison after ingesting the whole animal.

The coral snake is not a naturally aggressive animal and has a relatively small head but if molested, has a number of ruses to confound any predator. They may hide their heads under their bodies and flatten their tail and pretend that their tail is their head. They will thrash around and spasmodically crawl backwards and forwards and will even extrude sex organs as a defence pretence and sometimes feign death.

The relatively high fatality rate with coral snake bites may be due to their small heads and their habit of holding on and chewing. The poison is a neurotoxin and, should the worst happen, get the patient to the nearest medical centre as soon as possible. Do not cut and suck out the wound, do not catch the snake, it may bite again and even a severed head can inject venom. Do not bandage the limb so tight that the blood-flow is restricted. Give oxygen if there are any respiratory problems. Anti-venom treatment should only be given by an expert as it is itself dangerous and complicated and can have various side effects that themselves may need treating. The comment that if the bite doesn't kill you, the treatment might, is not totally untrue! Much more is now known about the treatment of bites and the first anti-venom laboratory in the area opened in Brazil in 1901 and is still a centre of excellence today. Of 7,562 patients treated with anti-venom there were only 181 deaths.

The woman who had rowed over in the canoe to Roberto's turned out to be looking for us. News, we were to discover, travels very quickly around these islands. It turned out that she was the real owner of the land with the little wooden shack and that the priest was a fiction. She and her sister had inherited it when their father had died and, they would like to sell it. We had been looking for something wildish where we could grow produce when we first decided to move to Central America but had not been able to find the right place at the right price. A bit of an island getaway did have a lot of appeal. One thing you have to be sure about when buying any property in Central America is that the title is right. So much land has been squatted on or confiscated by the government and then given away to people without a clear title that you can run into all kinds of problems. The Sandanista government confiscated a huge amount of property, much of which had been in the hands of the Somoza family. They did, after all, own 50% of all arable land in the country. Joe's first trip to Nicaragua in 1965 was to introduce mechanical cotton harvesters to the country, Somoza wanted him to work for him but even then Joe was told that if he ever wanted to live in Nicaragua it would not be advisable to be thought of as a "Somoza man". Joe did not take up the job offer. Senora Marta Pastor (this could be where the misunderstanding originated that a priest owned the land) said there was a small title problem in that she and her sister had never bothered to transfer the property into their names when their father had died. This, we were told, was a formality, just takes a couple of weeks and they needed to do it anyway. We said we would go and have another look at the property and see what we thought.

Back in the canoe but only after it had had a thorough washing to get rid of the copious amount of guano produced by the cormorants the previous night, the smell gently invading the whole area. The weather was still perfect and the plot of land nearby. I looked for the spoonbills that are meant to live here but none were to be seen, maybe they will be down the Rio Frio, which we wanted to explore later. Parrots were noisily flying in untidy groups from tree to tree and an osprey was perched on a branch. We passed the ranch house, which we now know is called the Hacienda Salvadora, and on around the bay to the small finca, El Tomate. We slowed down and took a look at the land. It was 20 manzanas (one manzana is 1.74 acres) about 200 metres lake frontage rising 171 metres to a wooded hilltop . It looked beautiful. We pulled into the dock area, disturbed a couple of wild ducks and tied up. Lava rocks everywhere.

"No wonder Roberto gave me a strange look when I asked him where he got his rocks." Joe murmured.

"No problem in getting hard core for a path."

We wandered around, trying hard not to get too enthusiastic and trying to be practical and objective. But....

"We could build a little house up there, it looks as though there might have been one there once."
"People say that there are still quite a few animals around here including deer and other mammals, possibly cats."

We were not sure that we believed these stories but on a trip that Joe made a few months later, he found the body of a deer on the bank where he had pulled up the canoe. Something had killed it and it probably wasn't a person as there were no gun wounds and nobody would have snared it and left it to rot without taking the meat. Some of the animal had been eaten including much of the stomach and a hind leg, the carcass looking similar to those left by the big cats in Kenya. Maybe a crocodile or caiman had caught it whilst it was drinking, but why hadn't they taken it off and, although there are meant to be plenty in the lake, we had not seen any to date. There was talk of jaguars……

There were plenty of fruit trees and plenty of space for more. A large number of young cedar trees had been planted and Joe set off to see if he could find any. I sat on a rock and gazed at the lake.

Joe returned from his clamber and told me that:

"The view from the top is spectacular, but probably too difficult to get to for a house. There are a couple of quite large fields under cultivation with beans and rice and the whole property is properly fenced, probably done when there were cattle here. We can find out more about it and we do not have to make any decisions now. Let's sleep on it."

Back at Roberto's, Joe and Roberto went off in the canoe to buy some cheese. We had discovered that Roberto had seen very little of the islands as he did not yet have his own boat. I settled down in a hammock with Tales from the Hills, now dried out, to enjoy the peace but I had hardly opened the book before I was asleep.

I woke up when Roberto and Joe came striding up the path, carrying a huge chunk of local cheese. Joe called to me to come down as we were going to the bar for a beer. What bar? A short trip over to the closest point on Isla Elvis Chavarria, about a kilometre, and there was a small hotel with cold beer and emerald green humming birds darting from one brilliant flower to another. We started talking about which flowers we could plant to attract them.

"We haven't bought it yet, and we may not buy it so don't get too enthusiastic."

"I know, but I can still think of what we might do with it?"

On their canoe trip Joe and Roberto had gone to the village and seen the man, Alfonso Arana, who makes the boats.   After discussions, a boat of 8 varras long and 46 inches wide made from cedro real would cost about US £500 and would take eight weeks to build.

"He wants half the money now to buy materials and the other half when it is finished, so I said that we would go over tomorrow with the first instalment."

We knew that we had to have a decent boat as the canoe was just not man enough for the lake, which was often windy and choppy.

We booked Sunday lunch at the hotel for the next day as, after two days of a diet of beans and rice, cheese and platano, something different would be welcome.   We bought some canned Victoria beers, wrapped them in newspapers to keep them cold and took them over to Atrevaesada, supper, fireflies, cormorants and bats

Next day we went over to the village with the money for the boat.   Alfonso, besides making boats also makes the traditional wooden houses with an open central area and a couple of rooms off on each side with large slatted windows. Very similar to the old dog-run Texan houses, both were designed to keep the air flowing.   There was a large screened veranda used for cooking and eating and lounging. Simple but functional, and at a cost of US$4,500, affordable. Perhaps we should build something like that?   Alfonso showed us a boat that he was building at the moment and said that as soon as it was finished, he would start on Joe's, once he had the permit for the wood.   There were many assurances that it would be well built, have a lifetime guarantee and be beautiful!   We bought some colourful balsa birds and strolled around the village.   Each gate had a sign saying 'artisan' to entice you in so we unlatched a gate and walked into a colourful abundant garden surrounding a house with a large porch on which people were working. We bought yet more birds and fish to hang in the Granada house for the anti-bat campaign there. They are exported all over the world and we see evidence of money being translated into decent housing, generators, some televisions, and boat engines, though not many as gasoline is an expense and has to come from San Carlos.

Our stay on Solentiname came to an abrupt end with a 4.30am alarm to catch the five o'clock boat to San Carlos. By the light of two torches we finished packing, cleaned teeth, fell over the canoe which Roberto had insisted that we leave in the bedroom where it would be locked up until Joe was back in three or four weeks, found our way to the kitchen and boiled some water for hot coffee. We now know that this is not really necessary as instant coffee is often just mixed with cold water and that is that. We now drink a lot of instant and cold though we do tend to add milk and perhaps sugar and perhaps a couple of large spoons of vanilla ice-cream, and maybe some coffee liqueur. Time was passing and we were gulping our coffee as we would have to negotiate the rather steep path to the dock in the pitch dark.

About 5.00am Roberto's workman appeared to help carry stuff down to the pier but, still, no Roberto. Eventually, Joe woke him and he appeared, quite relaxed, whilst we were panicking about missing the boat. We helped pack up hammocks, sort out bedding, tidy the kitchen and lock the rooms. Joe and I looked at each other, realisation dawning.

"It's the time change thing again, the boat has not changed its schedule, we are an hour early again."

Everything was on the jetty and we waited for the boat. The only way to catch the boat is to stand on your island and flash a torch and hope that the boat sees it. Roberto's relaxed morning, we discovered, was because he knew the schedule. The boat stayed in the bay on the next island and when it cranked its engine it was time to get up as he knew that he had 30 minutes before the boat reached hailing distance of Atrevesada. That morning the boat was late and there were torch lights on just about every island and it was nearly 6.00am (Nicaraguan time) before the boat headed towards our torch. It had already picked up eight people with all their stuff and empty gas tanks and water bottles for filling in San Carlos. In addition there were huge bags full of balsa animals. We packed our things away, including Roberto's generator, which refused to work, climbed over people, settled down and were off to the next flashlight. With amazing efficiency the boat pulled into docks, gravel beaches and grassy banks collecting people and more stuff. Everybody was going shopping. We looked around and already recognised some people, a man from the avocado farm, the girl who speaks English from the hotel, Senora Pastor going to sort out her land title. The last call and then 40 minutes to San Carlos, but everybody was already fast asleep.

Back at San Carlos and this time our adventure really was at an end. We said goodbye to Roberto collected our car, packed everything, including a bag of colourful balsa animals and set off along the road to Granada, but had left behind a boat being built and maybe a small finca.

Rio San Juan

Chapter 25   Papatura

We made a return trip to San Carlos and the Solentiname Islands in May the following year. A new, fast boat service had just started operation and was advertising Granada to San Carlos in four hours so we decided to try it. We were the only passengers, which might explain that it was out of business a few weeks later, but we did get to San Carlos far quicker.   A taxi over to the boat dock where Joe's Solentiname wooden boat was kept but it was looking rather sad as the paint had faded badly.   We threw our stuff on board, piled in, started the engine, now the 6hp, and moved away from the dock, past another pipe sticking out of the water from one of the steamships.   I picked up a plastic jug and started to bail the water out of the bottom of the boat.   I kept bailing and bailing and gradually realised that the water was rising quicker than I was throwing it out.

"Joe, we've got a problem. We're sinking!"

"Don't be ridiculous, of course we aren't"

"We are, I can see holes between the boards, we are going to have to go into shore.   Look."   I pointed at the water bubbling into the boat.

"OK, keep bailing and I'll take it into the bank next to the transporter boats, we can get it fixed there."

We pulled onto the bank and threw our bags onto the bank to try to keep them dry and inspected the boat.   There were huge gaps between the planks where caulking had come loose.   The family with whom Joe had left the canoe had promised that they would take good care of it and cover it with palm leaves to keep the sun off.   Had they?   As Joe said, "hell no."

The wood had been allowed to get really dry, had shrunk and out had popped the caulking. San Carlos on an Easter weekend was completely dead, nobody around except for a few local drunks being carted off by wheelbarrow to the local communal washing area to sleep it off. I went to find help but the girl tending the only shop open and the couple of men talking with her just shook their heads and said that nobody would be doing any work for the next three days. I reported this unhelpful news to Joe and that either we had to do something or we were stuck in San Carlos for three days. By now Joe was already busy. He had picked up some fabric lying around, had torn it into strips and was stuffing it into the cracks – instant caulking!

Things change very quickly in Nicaragua and San Carlos was showing improvements in the relatively short time between our visits. There were new cobbles on many of the streets, the fish vendors by the ferry-boats had been moved, streets were much, much cleaner. There was a new hostel and the restaurant was having a complete make-over, but, even so, three days would be a long time to stay.

"It will be all right. Help me push it back into the water and let's go."

It was not perfect but Joe thought it would get us to Solentiname. We only had the box and a couple of bags with us and we balanced these on some boards to keep them out of the water in the bottom of the boat and started out. We now had two bailing jugs and it was soon obvious that, again, we were not winning against the water.

"See if you can see where it is coming in."

"Everywhere" was my first unhelpful comment, but then "between the third and fourth planks near the front."

"OK, you take the tiller, keep following the buoys and I'll see what I can do."

We changed places and I grabbed the tiller and kept to the marked channel.

"It is not just a crack, there is a hole here but I think that I can plug it well enough to get us to the islands."

Some more stuffing of holes then we changed places again. I kept bailing but was now more than keeping up with the water.

"We will be all right getting to Solentiname and first thing tomorrow I'll see if we can get a temporary repair and then I will leave the boat to get it done properly when we leave. I can collect it in a couple of weeks when I have to come back."

The boat did make it to the islands and we beached it next to one of the small hotels for the night. We hoped that Alfonso would be around to repair it as he was a Seventh day Adventist preacher and kept different religious days than the Catholics and non-conformists. We found him working on another boat and he agreed to make a temporary repair that would get us to Papatura and then he would do a proper job when we left it with him.

"Let's go and look at the finca and then we can keep going across the lake to Papatura on the mainland and see if they are having the rodeo.

There were two main reasons why we had made this trip. Joe had had numerous telephone conversations with Marta, her lawyer in San Carlos and ours in Granada about buying the finca. He had made half a dozen trips to San Carlos and Solentiname and had still not seen hide nor sight of the title. After nine months, with promises every month that there was no problem we will have the title next week, we had decided that there was, possibly, no title, to the property. We had both cooled on buying the finca as, when things become too difficult it is often just not worthwhile continuing, and there seemed to be serious disagreements within the family.   On one trip to the finca with some members of the family, Joe said that the arguing was so bad that he eventually just got into the boat and left everybody there as he thought that it was going to turn into a full scale fist fight.

"I don't think I want to get involved with this." He told me on his return to Granada.

But Marta was insistent that everything would be all right and we decided to make one last trip.   We pulled onto the small beach, jumped into the water and pulled the boat onto the stones.   No worry about leaving the boat it was absolutely flat calm.

" I want to walk up the path to as high a point as we can easily reach and then back, down along the fence line as I don't really understand exactly where it goes."   Joe explained.

We set off past the lower fruit trees, through some scrub up to some larger, older trees.   We were absolutely shocked to see that two of these trees had been completely ringed, the bark removed in a circle around the whole circumference of the trunks so that they would die.

"He's been told that he cannot come on this land any more and cut trees and he does this."   Joe stated, sad for the trees but angry.

He, was a relation of Marta's who, along with his wife, had been coming up with all kinds of 'deals' about the land.

Joe was furious, appalled by the waste of such beautiful trees for no other purpose than firewood or a not so subtle way of persuading us not to buy the property.

"The only good thing is that it was only two trees." Joe mutters.

I am not so sanguine, too many things were going wrong.

We had a quick picnic and a swim in water that was as hot as a bath and not really that pleasant but it was nice to get wet and a little cool when standing in the air.

Back in the boat we set forth for Papatura and the Los Guatuzos Reserve and, perhaps, the second reason for our trip, the rodeo.

Joe had gone over to Papatura in the silver canoe the previous year to see the river and the reserve and discovered that the rodeo was on at the same time. Three days of non-stop music, dancing, cowboys, horses and bulls. The town was swarming with people arriving by bus, taxi, boat, horse and on foot. There were bars and restaurants, instant shops selling clothes, electronics (this in a town with no electricity), shoes and boots, hats and jeans. At 50 cordobas a day (about 2.8 US dollars) it was expensive for an average Nicaraguan but every day the ring was full and, though small by American standards, it held 400 people and everyone had a close-up seat.

Like the Texas rodeo this was serious business with three days of bull riding; the twenty or so candidates riding once each day with the competition starting just after noon to finish before sundown. There were professional judges and prize money. The bulls were from Costa Rica and were strong and full-grown, full of fight, snorting and pawing and leaping when released into the ring, dust flying as the riders fought to stay on board. There were two 'clowns' to protect any riders from getting gored and to encourage the bulls but they were so brave and outrageous that even they had to be restrained, just like the boys who tried to get into the bull pens at the end of each day. The noise from the crowd was terrific as they cheered on their favourite rider, money changing hands. The competition was so intense that, after one rodeo not long before, the winner was stabbed to death by a losing contestant.

Joe said that the three days he was there was just a blur of noise, day and night.

We crossed the lake, somewhat surprised when half way over we bumped into something underwater, thankfully not hard. We had absolutely no idea what it was and continued onto the mainland.

"We are looking for a house with an antenna right on the water, the entrance to the river is near there." Joe instructed.

I spotted two possible buildings and we headed for the nearest which turned out to be a ranch so we followed the coast towards the second.

"This is the right place, we now have to find the entrance."

A couple of false starts and then we saw it, narrow and not clogged and we nosed into a beautiful small river. This area of Nicaragua has an extremely interesting and complex eco-system as it has dry and wet forest, swamps, 12 rivers and has been called the cradle of life for the lake. It is a major bird nesting area and you can see the jabiru stork here, a spectacular bird, 135 centimetres tall with white plumage, a black head and a bright red bib. The literature suggests that caimans, crocodiles and alligators are all present in the lake and rivers and caiman and turtle eggs are collected by the Guatuzos research station, where they are hatched and the young reared until they are strong enough to be released back into the wild. There are over 130 orchids, 389 birds, 81 amphibia, 136 reptiles and 42 mammals including sloths, jaguars and anteaters. The whole water system is a nursery for the lake and river fishes including the ancient, armoured, gaspar.

This whole area was only explored in the later 1800s when people were looking for rubber, then slaves and later, cacao. The whole area became pretty much depopulated in the 1980s during a border dispute with Costa Rica.

Thomas Belt tells:

"that the first people who ascended the Rio Frio (a nearby river) were attacked by the Indians who killed several with their arrows. The ferocity and accuracy of the Indians might have led to the river remaining unexplored for much longer had it not been for the rubber trade. Rubber collectors had to move further afield and the Rio Frio gave access to a new area and the, now armed, collectors easily outmatched the Indians with their spears, and bows and arrows. The Indians ran whenever they saw a boat which was then left to plunder their villages take their crops and sometimes, even their children."

The river was beautiful, plenty of birds, shade from the trees and the plopping of fish and turtles slipping into the water on our approach. We see a gently sloping riverbank ahead and think 'caiman' and, as if on cue, there was the largest caiman I had ever seen. About nine feet long he was inert in a patch of sunlight and further on, two more were lazing half out of the water. No swimming in this water.

We had tried to find out if they were holding the rodeo this year but even after all our phonecalls, had not managed to discover anything. Four kilometres down the river we tied up at the research station/hostel and arranged a bed for the night, but were warned that there was no food. But that was all right, we would find something in the village so we strolled down the path and into the tiny town; a kapok tree had spilt its down over the path so it was like walking on a silken carpet. The one restaurant was closed and there were only a dozen houses and absolutely no rodeo. The rodeo ring still there but covered with weeds and clearly hadn't been used since Joe's last trip. We asked at one house if there was another restaurant anywhere and are told that if we come back at about 6.00 that evening, they would have some food for us and "didn't you come in the silver canoe last year?" Everybody remembered the crazy gringo in the canoe!

We strolled back to the lodge and walked to the forest past the butterfly farm, the baby caiman and turtles and through the orchid farm. Howler monkeys were seemingly everywhere in the trees and later that evening, at dusk, a whole family camped for the night in the trees overhanging our boat. They lay along the branches, completely relaxed, with legs dangling. A walkway had been built through the trees in the forest about 40 feet above the ground so we climbed the ladder to the start of the first leg. This should be good, I thought, being up in the trees. Joe went first, the whole span shaking and I followed about a dozen paces behind and then, I stopped. It was steel mesh hung on cables with one cable as a handrail to hang onto on each side and only one other cable between that and the walkway. There was absolutely nothing to keep you from falling should you slip. The further along you went, the more it swung. I hated it, Joe just thought that I was a sissy and was completely unsympathetic but all I wanted was to get back onto the ground.

We showered and walked over to the house/restaurant but were stopped by the police before we got there and asked for our boat papers, which of course, we did not have. Twenty cordobas later, whether paid as a fine or a permit, we never discovered but which seemed to solve the problem, we went on to our candlelit, mosquito infested supper, which was actually rather good. The mosquitoes were strange as they were a real problem to everybody, and there must have been about 12 people staying in the house, but two hours later there was hardly one to be heard, seen or felt! We asked about the rodeo and were told that permission had not been given for the bulls to come from Costa Rica so, as there were no suitable bulls in this part of Nicaragua, no rodeo. We sauntered back to the lodge, spotting the eyes of caimans everywhere along the river -banks.

Joe was amazed at the town when there was no rodeo.

"There is just nothing here. No wonder they made such a big thing of it as it must be the only event of the year and now it has been stopped. Probably something to do with the long-running squabble with Costa Rica about the border."

Next morning we strolled in the forest again and then left in the boat back to the lake and Solentiname. We wriggled down the river and pulled over to let the weekly shopping boat to San Carlos pass, no sign of caimans, where were they? Slowly we reached the lake and headed out to the islands. Another ferry-boat from San Carlos was heading for the river and as they waved to us, we waved back and then, another crunch as the boat hit something in the water at about the same place as before.

"They weren't just waving, they were trying to tell us that we were heading for rocks or something. I wonder why whatever it is is not marked?"

There was certainly something in the water here and we were lucky that the water was deep enough but we never discovered what the obstruction was. There are plenty of shipping hazards in the lake but, as most people who use the lake have been born on it, you are expected to just, know.

We reached the islands and left the boat for re-caulking and painting at Alfonso's, near our hotel. There, Joe was met by the elderly relatives of Marta.

"We have decided that we are going to keep half a manzana of the finca for our beans."

Joe is flabbergasted.

"No, we have already talked about this, the property has to be sold entire, all trees, all land and the house or I am not interested."

The couple insist that, as the property is being sold as 20 manzanas, when it is actually 20 and ½ manzanas, they want the half, the bean patch in the middle of the land. So Joe just said:

"I quit, the deal is off."

We talked about it over a beer that evening and discovered that we were both quite relieved that we had decided not to go ahead. There were more people involved than we had initially been led to believe, Joe was already furious with the old man for cutting trees and now, ringing others. Joe also told me that he had seen a snake in the house. Now I am not neurotic about snakes but it just happens that every tropical property I have tried to buy where I have seen a snake, has fallen through or led to a disaster, so I tend to think of them as omens!

"I do not want to buy it any more, I think that there will be continual problems."

I agreed with Joe.

Next morning we took the ferry to San Carlos and in the afternoon, the old overnight boat to Granada packed with crates of fish, that would be on sale in Miami the next afternoon, and buckets of cheese. The trip was an experience in itself and the very first thing was to find a space to hang your hammock as this becomes your area and the only place to sit as the air conditioned lounge is too cold and, anyway, all the seats have been bagged for the night. You sat or lay and read until it was too dark and then tried to sleep. There were three stops on the way where goods and people were loaded and unloaded and hawkers tried to sell you food and drinks. In Morito cheeses, some of which had been delivered to the quay on horses, were carefully put on the boat in the middle of the night, just like those put into Squier's bongo. Some things have hardly changed. Much of the time you just lay and watched the stars with the gentle roll of the boat. Early in the morning we were at Granada, and home.

The final end to this story comes later that week when Joe returns to Solentiname to pick up his re-caulked and newly re-painted red and green boat. The weather was exceptionally calm and Joe decided to take the boat up the lake to Granada, which he did, taking two days and some anxious moments with the erratic conditions in the lake and which is a story all of its own. Before leaving Solentiname he went past the finca, one more time, just to see how he felt. There was a slight drizzle and Joe's glasses had water drops on them. Something looked different. He took his glasses off, wiped them, put them back on, settled them on his nose, and stared, not believing what he saw, or rather, what he does not see. The house had completely gone, even the cement wood stove. Not a piece of anything left standing!

Joe tells me about it back in Granada.

"Well it was an experience but there is absolutely no way that I would buy it now." The sad thing is that everyone lost out. Marta did not get her money so that she could go and buy something in Chontales. The old couple did not get their money that would have allowed them to buy their own bean field and a new house. We did not get our fruit finca.

" I am sure it was the right decision not to buy it and getting there was always going to be difficult, even with the new road and the new boat. I was talking with a friend yesterday, have you ever thought about having a small coffee farm?"

Rio San Juan

Addendum

After the decision not to pursue the finca on Solentiname, we did go and look at coffee farms as we were interested in a small agricultural enterprise. We found a beautiful farm near Jinotega in Nicaragua, and although it was somewhat run down it had a large nursery of young plants, was shaded by magnificent, very old, forest trees and had a small river running through it so there was plenty of water. It was on our second visit, when we were being taken around the perimeter of the farm, walking on steep hillsides, that Joe had his first indication that all was not well and said that he did not think that he could make it to the end of the trail.

Shortly afterwards Joe was diagnosed with prostate cancer. Joe decided that he wanted to return to his ranch in Texas for whatever time was available to him where he received the best possible care and treatment from the dedicated people at the Veterans Association Hospital at Temple, Texas and later from the Hospice nurses. Joe died on almost the exact spot that he was born.

Joe had been in the US coastguard, worked in the oil industry, was a rancher/farmer working the farm that his father created, started a cable television business, owned a race-track, and built a roller skating rink for the children in the small town where he lived. He had been involved in a number of other enterprises but when he was 50, he decided to take up ballooning and spent the next 20 years flying commercial and passenger balloons all over the world. He was an inveterate traveller and amongst many other trips explored much of Europe from Spain to Italy, Greece, and Turkey and then Egypt, Jordan, Israel, and Lebanon, all on his Vespa. I met Joe in Kenya and after 5 years with Joe flying balloons over the Masai Mara game reserve, Joe retired and we took our Landrover on a trip from Nairobi to Eritrea and Ethiopia and then around south and east Africa to Cape Town and back to Nairobi before we decided to settle in Granada, Nicaragua.

The Rio San Juan trip was just one of many adventures that we had together and I treasure every day of the wild adventure that was life with Joe Brown.

Meanwhile, the Rio San Juan keeps flowing down to the sea though now Costa Rica has built a road on the south bank of the river between El Castillo and Bartola and a bridge is being constructed across the river from San Carlos. Maybe there will be more travellers who will have their own tales to tell of the Rio San Juan.

Appendix I

The Monroe Doctrine

In the wars of the European Powers, in matters relating to themselves, we have never taken any part, nor does it comport with our policy to do so. It is only when our rights are invaded or seriously menaced that we resent injuries or make preparation for our defense. With the movements in this hemisphere we are of necessity more immediately connected and by causes which must be obvious to all enlightened citizens and impartial observers.

We owe it therefore to candor, and to the amicable relations between the United States and those powers, to declare that we should consider any attempt on their part to extend their system to any portion of this hemisphere as dangerous to our peace and safety. With the existing colonies or dependencies of any European Power we have not interfered and shall not interfere. But with the governments who have declared their independence and maintained it, and whose independence we have on great consideration and on just principles, acknowledged, we could not view any interposition for the purpose of oppressing them, or controlling in any other manner, their destiny, by any European Power, in any other light than as the manifestation of an unfriendly disposition toward the United States. In the war between these new governments and Spain we declared our neutrality at the time of their recognition, and to this we have adhered and shall continue to adhere, providing no change shall occur which, in the judgment of the competent authorities of this government, shall make a corresponding change on the part of the United States indispensable to their security.

It is impossible that the Allied Powers should extend their political system to any portion of either continent without endangering our peace and happiness; nor can anyone believe that our Southern brethren, if left to themselves, would adopt it of their own accord. It is equally impossible therefore, that we should behold such interposition, in any form, with indifference.

Appendix II

The American Atlantic and Pacific Ship Canal Company contract

"It is and has been stipulated, by and between the high contracting parties –

"1st. That the citizens, vessels, and merchandise of the United States shall enjoy in all the ports and harbors of Nicaragua, upon both oceans, a total exemption from all port-charges, tonnage or anchorage duties, or any other similar charges now existing, or which may hereafter be established, in manner the same as it said ports had been declared Free Ports. And it is further stipulated, that the right of way or transit across the territories of Nicaragua, by any route or upon any mode of communication at present existing, or which may hereafter be constructed, shall at all times be open and free to the Government and citizens of the United States, for all lawful purposes whatever; and no tolls, duties, or charges of any kind shall be imposed upon the transit in whole or part, by such modes of communication, of vessels of war, or other property belonging to the Government of the United States, or on public mails sent under the authority of the same, or upon persons in its employ, nor upon citizens of the United States, nor upon vessels belonging to them. And it is also stipulated that all lawful produce, manufactures, merchandise, or other property belonging to citizens of the United States, passing from one ocean to the other in either direction, for the purpose of exportation to foreign countries, shall not be subject to any import or export duties whatever; or if citizens of the United States, having introduced such produce, manufactures, or merchandise into the State of Nicaragua, for sale or exchange, shall, within three years thereafter, determine to export the same, they shall be entitled to drawback equal to four fifths of the amount of duties paid upon their importation.

"2nd. And inasmuch as a contract was entered into on the twenty-seventh day of August, 1849 between the Republic of Nicaragua and a company of citizens of the United States, styles the 'American Atlantic and Pacific Ship Canal Company,' and in order to secure the construction and permanence of the great work thereby contemplated, both high contracting parties do severally and jointly agree to protect and defend the above-named Company in the full and perfect enjoyment of said work, from its inception to is completion, and after its completion, from any acts of invasion, forfeiture, or violence, from whatever quarter the same may proceed; and to give full effect to the stipulations here made, and to secure for the benefit of mankind the uninterrupted advantages of such communication from sea to sea, the United States distinctly recognizes the rights of sovereignty and property which the State of Nicaragua possesses in and over the line of said canal, and for the same reason guaranties, positively and efficaciously, the entire neutrality of the same, so long as it shall remain under the control of citizens of the United States, and so long as the United States shall enjoy the privileges secured to them in the preceding section of this article.

"3rd. But if, by any contingency, the above-named American Atlantic and Pacific Ship Canal Company' shall fail to comply with the terms of their contract with the State of Nicaragua, all the rights and privileges which said contract confers shall accrue to any Company of citizens of the United States which shall, within one year after the official declaration of failure, undertake to comply with its provisions, so far as the same may at that time be applicable, provided the company thus assuming said contract shall first present to the President and Secretary of State of the United States satisfactory assurances of their intention and ability to comply with the same; of which satisfactory assurances the

Rio San Juan

signature of the Secretary of State and the seal of the Department shall be complete evidence.

"4th. And it is also agreed, on the part of the Republic of Nicaragua, that none of the rights, privileges, and immunities guarantied, and by the preceding articles, but especially by the first section of this article, conceded to the United States and its citizens, shall accrue to any other nation, or to its citizens, except such nation shall first enter into the same treaty stipulations, for the defence and protection of the proposed great interoceanic canal, which have been entered into by the United States,

in terms the same with those embraced in section 2d of this article."

Appendix III

Clayton-Bulwer Treaty of April, 1850

Article I

The governments of the United States and Great Britain herby declare that neither the one nor the other will ever obtain or maintain for itself any exclusive control over the said ship canal; agreeing that neither will ever erect or maintain any fortifications commanding the same, or in the vicinity thereof, or occupy, or fortify, or colonize, or assume, or exercise any dominion over Nicaragua, Costa Rica, the Mosquito coast, or any part of Central America; nor will either make use of any protection which either affords or may afford, or any alliance which either has or may have to or with any state or people, for the purpose of erecting or maintaining any such fortifications, or of occupying, fortifying, or colonizing Nicaragua, Costa Rica, the Mosquito coast, or any part of Central America, or of assuming or exercising dominion over the same; nor will the United States of Great Britain take advantage of any intimacy, or us any alliance, connection or influence that either may possess with any State or Government through whose territory the said can may pass, for the purpose of acquiring or holding, directly or indirectly, for the citizens of subjects of the one, any rights or advantages in regard to commerce or navigation through the said canal which shall not be offered on the same terms to the citizens or subjects of the other.

Article II

Vessels of the United States or Great Britain traversing the said canal shall, in case of war between the contracting

Rio San Juan

parties, be exempted from blockade, detention or capture by either of the belligerents; and this provision shall extend to such a distance from the two ends of the said canal as may hereafter be found expedient to establish.

Article III

In order to secure the construction of the said canal, the contracting parties engage that if any such canal shall be undertaken upon fair and equitable terms by any parties having the authority of the local Government or Governments through whose territory the same may pass, then the persons employed in making the said canal, and their property used, or to be used, for that object, shall be protected, from the commencement of the said canal to its completion, by the Governments of the United States and Great Britain, from unjust detention, confiscation, seizure or any violence whatsoever.

Article IV

The contracting parties will use whatever influence they respectively exercise with any State, States, or Governments possessing or claiming to possess any jurisdiction or right over the territory which the said canal shall traverse, or which shall be near the waters applicable thereto, in order to induce such States or Governments to facilitate the construction of the said canal by every means in their power. And furthermore, the United States and Great Britain agree to use their good offices, wherever or however it may be most expedient, in order to procure the establishment of two free ports, one at each end of the said canal.

Article V

The contracting parties further engage, that when the said canal shall have been completed, they will protect it from interruption, seizure or unjust confiscation, and that they will guarantee the neutrality thereof, so that the said canal may forever be open and free, and the capital invested therein secure. Nevertheless, the Governments of the United States and Great Britain, in according their protection to the construction of the said canal, and guaranteeing its neutrality and security when completed, always understand that this protection and guarantee are granted conditionally, and may be withdrawn by both Governments, or either Government, if both Governments, or either Government, should deem that the persons or company undertaking or managing the same adopt or establish such regulations concerning the traffic thereupon as are contrary to the spirit and intention of this convention, either by making unfair discriminations in favor of the commerce of one of the contracting parties over the commerce of the other, or by imposing oppressive exactions or unreasonable tolls upon the passengers, vessels, goods, wares, merchandise or other articles. Neither party, however, shall withdraw the aforesaid protection and guarantee without first giving six months notice to the other.

Article VI

The contracting parties in this convention engage to invite every State with which both or either have friendly intercourse to enter into stipulations with them similar to those which they have entered into with each other, to the end that all other States may share in the honor and advantage of having contributed to a work of such general interest and importance as the canal herein contemplated. And the contracting parties likewise agree that each shall enter into treaty stipulations with such of the Central American States as they may deem advisable, for the purpose of more effectually carrying out the great design of this convention, namely, that of constructing and maintaining the said canal as a ship communication between the two oceans for the benefit of mankind, on equal terms to all, and of protecting the same; and they also agree that the good offices of either shall be employed, when requested by the other, in aiding and assisting the negotiation of such treaty stipulations; and should any differences arise as to right or property over the territory through which the said canal shall pass between the States or Governments of Central America, and such differences should in any way impede or obstruct the execution of the said canal, the Governments of the United States and Great Britain will use their good offices to settle such differences in the manner best suited to promote the interests of the said canal, and to strengthen the bonds of friendship and alliance which exist between the contracting parties.

Article VII

It being desirable that no time should be unnecessarily lost in commencing and constructing the said canal, the Governments of the United States and Great Britain determine to give their support and encouragement to such persons or company as may first offer to commence the same, with the necessary capital, the consent of the local authorities, and on such principles as accord with the spirit and intention of this convention; and it any persons or company should already have, with any State through which the proposed ship canal may pass, a contract for the construction of such a canal as that specified in the convention, to the stipulations of which contract neither of the contracting parties in this convention have any just cause to object, and the said persons or company shall moreover have made preparations and expended time, money and trouble on the faith of such contract, it is hereby agreed that such persons or company shall have a priority of claim over every other person, persons, or company to the protection of the Governments of the United States and Great Britain, and be allowed a year from the date of the exchange of the ratifications of this convention for concluding their arrangements, and presenting evidence of sufficient capital subscribed to accomplish the contemplated undertaking; it being understood that if, at the expiration of the aforesaid period, such persons or company be not able to commence and carry out the proposed enterprise, then the Governments of the United States and Great Britain shall be free to afford their protection to any other persons or company that shall be prepared to commence and proceed with the construction of the canal in question.

Article VIII

The Governments of the United States and Great Britain having not only desired, in entering into this convention, to accomplish a particular object, but also to establish a general principle, they hereby agree to extend their protection, by treaty stipulations, to any other practicable communications, whether by canal or railway, across the isthmus which connects North and South America, and especially to the interoceanic communications, should the same prove to be practicable, whether by canal or railway, which are now proposed to be established by the way of Tehuantepec or Panama. In granting, however, their joint protection to any such canals or railways as are by this article specified, it is always understood by the United States and Great Britain that the parties constructing or owning the same shall impose no other charges or conditions of traffic thereupon than the aforesaid Governments shall approve of as just and equitable; and that the same canals or railways, being open to the citizens and subjects of the United States and Great Britain on equal terms, shall also be open on the like terms to the citizens and subjects of every other State which is willing to grant thereto such protection as the United States and Great Britain engage to afford.

Article IX

The ratifications of this convention shall be exchanged at Washington within six months from this day, or sooner if possible.

In faith whereof we, the respective plenipotentiaries, have signed this convention and have hereunto affixed our seals.

Done at Washington the nineteenth day of April, anno Domini one thousand eight hundred and fifty.

John M Clayton
Henry Lytton Bulwer

Bibliography

Aguirre Sacasa, Francisco Xavier Nicaragua and Historical Atlas. Coleccion Cultural de Centro America 2002

Allen, Merritt Parmelee William Walker Filibuster. New York and London: Harper and Brothers 1932

Belt, Thomas The Naturalist in Nicaragua. University of Chicago Press, 1985

Boyle, Frederick A Ride Across a Contine ss 1985nt: A personal Narrative of Wanderings through Nicaragua and Costa Rica Vols I-II. London: Richard Bentley 1868

Bransford, J.F. Archaeological Researches in Nicaragua. Annual Report of the Smithsonian Institution 1881 (Printed 1882)

Butterworth, Hezekiah Lost in Nicaragua. Boston: W.A. Wilde 1898

Campbell, Jonathan A. and Lamar, William W. The Venemous Reptiles of the Western Hemisphere, Cornell University Press 2004

Carr, Albert Z.Gree The World and William Walker. New York: Harper and Row 1963

Carr, Archie High Jungles and Low. Gainesville: University of Florida Press 1953

Colquohoun, Archibald Ross The Key of the Pacific: The Nicaraguan Canal. Westminster: Archibald Constable and Company 1895

Columbus, Christopher translated By Cecil Jane The Journal of Christopher Columbus. New York: Bonanza Books 1989

Cordingly, David Under the Black Flag. New York: Random House 1995

De Leeuw, Hendrik Crossroads of the Buccaneeers. Philadelphia: J.B. Lippincott Company 1937

Doubleday, C.W. Reminiscences of the "Filibuster" War in Nicaragua. New York and London: C.P. Putnam's Sons 1886

Dunlop, Robert Glasgow Travels in Central America, Being a Journey of Nearly Three Years Residence in the Country. London: Longman, Brown, Green, and Longmans, 1847

Esquemeling, John The Buccaneers of America: A True Account of the Most Remarkable Assaults Committed of Late Years upon the Coasts of the West Indies by the Buccaneers of Jamaica and Tortuga. London: George Aallen and Unwin, Ltd 1951

Firstbrook, Peter   The Voyage of the Matthew. London: BBC Books 1997

Green, Lawrence   The Filibuster. The Career of William Walker. New York: Bobbs-Merrill Company 1937

Jamison, James Caarson   With Walker in Nicaragua. Columbia: E.W. Stephens Publishing Company 1909

Janzen, Daniel H. ed. Costa Rican Natural History. Chicago: The University of Chicago Press 1983

LaFeber, Walter   The Panama Canal. The Crisis in Historical Perspective. New York: Oxford University Press 1978

Lambert, Andrew   Nelson. Britannia's God of War. London: Faber and Faber 2004

Lewis, Oscar   Sea Routes to the Gold Fields. The Migration by Water to California in 1849-1852. New York: Knopf 1949

Lucas, Daniel B.   Nicaragua: War of the Filibusters. Richmond: B.F. Johnson Publishing Company 1896

Marriot, Edward   Savage Shore, Life and Death with Nicaragua's Last Shark Hunters. Owl Books 2001

Miller, Hugh Gordon The Isthmian Highway. New York: The Macmillan Company 1929

Morison, Samuel Eliot Admiral of the Ocean Sea. A Life of Christopher Colombus. Boston: Little, Brown and Company 1942

Newton, Norman Thomas Gage in Spanish America. New York: Barnes and Noble 1969

Parker, Franklin D., ed. Travels in Central America 1821-1840. Gainesville: University of Florida Press 1970

Pim, Bedford The Gate of the Pacific. London: Lovell Reeve and Company 1863

Pim, Bedford and Seemann, Berthold Dottings on the Roadside, in Panama, Nicaragua and Mosquito. London: Chapman and Hall 1869

Roberts, Orlando W. Narrative of Voyages and Excursions on the Est Coast and in The Interior of Central America; Describing a Journey Up The River San Juan, and Passage Across the Lade of Nicaragua to the City of Leon. Gainesville: University of Florida Press 1965

Squiers, Ephraim George Nicaragua: Its People, Scenery, Monuments, Resources, Conditions and Proposed Canal. Revised ed: New York: Harper and Brothers 1860

Twain, Mark Travels with Mr. Brown. New York: Knopf 1940

Walker, William The War in Nicaragua. Mobile: S.H. Goetzel, 1860

Wells, William Vincent Walker's expedition to Nicaragua, a History of the Central American War and the Sonora and Kinney Expeditions. New York: Stringer and Townsend 1856

Williams, Max Harrison Gateway Through Central America. A History of the San Juan River – Lake Nicaragua Waterway 1502-1976. Empreza Editoria "Urquizo Ltda" La Paz, Bolivia 1976

Worth, Joseph Adventures and Narrow Escapes in Nicaragua. San Francisco: Spaulding and Barto Books and Job Printing 1872

Printed in Great Britain
by Amazon.co.uk, Ltd.,
Marston Gate.